DATE DUE

MAY 1 4	MAR 1 2	JUN 1
	JUN 1 8	DEC 9 '87
JUL 12	FEB 11 '81	JUN 8 '88
DEC 3	MAR 1 '8	JUN 2 5 '89
FEB 11	MAR 17	FEB 1 5 '89
MAR 24 '76	OCT 13 '8	MAR 8 '99
JUN 2 3	DEC	JAN 31 '90
FEB 22 78	FEB 9 '83	MAR 1 4 '90
MAR 1 5 78	MAR 9 '8	APR 4 '90
FEB 7 '80	JUN 23 85	15 9
	FEB 1 8 87	MAY 24 90

Martin Luther

PRAEGER PATHFINDER BIOGRAPHIES

ARISTOTLE:

Founder of Scientific Philosophy
by Benjamin Farrington

CHARLES DARWIN:

Pioneer in the Theory of Evolution
by H. E. L. Mellersh

MOHAMMED:

Prophet of the Religion of Islam
by E. Royston Pike

Martin Luther

LEADER OF THE REFORMATION

LEONARD W. COWIE

FREDERICK A. PRAEGER, *Publishers*
New York • Washington

BOOKS THAT MATTER

Published in the United States of America in 1969
by Frederick A. Praeger, Inc., Publishers
111 Fourth Avenue, New York, N.Y. 10003

Library of Congress Catalog Card Number: 69–12703

Printed in the United States of America

Contents

1 Luther's Germany   3

2 Schoolboy and Student   15

3 The Troubled Friar   26

4 The Question of Indulgences   37

5 The Diet of Worms   52

6 Turmoil and Conflict   64

7 The Lutheran Church   77

8 Catechism and Hymns   89

9 Marriage and Later Years   101

10 Epilogue   113

THE MAIN EVENTS IN LUTHER'S LIFE   118

SUGGESTIONS FOR FURTHER READING   120

INDEX   121

List of Illustrations

Map of sixteenth-century Europe 5
Map of the Holy Roman Empire 7
Luther's parents 17
Luther as a friar 28
Wittenberg 30
Tetzel 41
Pope Leo X 47
Emperor Charles V 55
Wartburg Castle 61
Luther—a contemporary portrait 70
Peasants attacking a monastery 72
Erasmus 75
Zwingli 83
Melanchthon 87
Luther preaching 91
Luther and Huss 93
Manuscript of the hymn "A Safe Stronghold" 98
Catherine von Bora 102
Courtyard of the Augustinian priory at Wittenberg 105

Martin Luther

I

Luther's Germany

In 1521, King Henry VIII of England published a book under
his own name in which he condemned the religious ideas of a
German friar. The book was called *A Defence of the Seven
Sacraments Against Martin Luther*. The King presented a
copy, bound in gold, to the Pope, who rewarded him with the
title of *"Fidei Defensor"* ("Defender of the Faith"), a title
(abbreviated to *"Fid. Def."*) that appears after the sovereign's
name on old British coins.

By this time, a number of Luther's books had already
reached England. Many were seized by royal officials and publicly burned in front of St. Paul's Cathedral in London; others
were discovered in Cambridge and burned there, on the Market Hill. But people in England continued to read Luther's
books. In Cambridge itself, a little group of scholars from several of the colleges met regularly at the White Horse Inn to
discuss Luther's teachings. Among these young men, who

slipped through a side entrance into the back room of the inn, were William Tyndale, who was to translate the Bible into English, Thomas Cranmer and Matthew Parker, who were to become archbishops of Canterbury, and other young men destined to become bishops. Several in the group were later to be burned at the stake for their religious views. In the days of Henry VIII, however, these young men were just beginning to develop their ideas, and they were learning from Luther. The townspeople of Cambridge nicknamed them the "Germans" and the White Horse Inn, "Little Germany."

The copies of Luther's books that reached England had, most likely, been hidden in ships' cargoes and smuggled into the country by German merchants. In Henry VIII's reign, other east-coast English towns, such as King's Lynn, Norwich, Yarmouth, and Ipswich, did much trading with the towns of northern Germany. Indeed, Germany was at this time the center of European trade. In the north, the Hanse, an economic league of northern German towns, dominated the commerce of the Baltic and the North Sea, while in the south, the towns on the Rhine and the Danube controlled the valuable trade routes that led across the Alps into Italy, and from France and Burgundy in the west to Germany's prospering industries and markets in the east.

Germany's rich mineral resources made possible a profitable mining industry—which included the copper mines that brought Luther's father his wealth—and provided raw material for the prospering metal and armament manufactures. German financial firms were also flourishing, especially those controlled by the two great rival banking families the Fuggers and the Welsers, who were both of the city of Augsburg. Germany's production and trade were stimulated by the rise in prices throughout western Europe. This general inflation

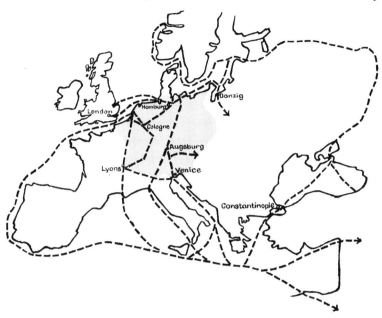

The position of Germany in Europe and the major trade routes in the early sixteenth century

resulted from the growing import of bullion from the Spanish mines in the New World.

Germans were active not only in trade and industry but also in the arts. This was the age of artists like Albrecht Dürer and Lucas Cranach, who both came to sympathize with Luther's religious views. The revolutionary invention of printing had recently been made in Germany, and the country now had many presses—which, indeed, helped spread Luther's ideas. Finally, there was a great demand for education, especially in the towns; Germany had more universities and more students than any other country in Europe. Nine new German universities were founded between 1450 and 1517; among these was the University of Wittenberg, where Luther taught. The Lutherans were to establish six more during the sixteenth century. As a historian recently said, "Luther's Germany was in many ways the most alive, the most flourishing part of Europe."

Politically, Germany was divided into many separate parts, and no single German state was as powerful as the kingdom of England, France, or Spain. Twelve million Germans lived in some 350 separate political realms of varying sizes. Some were states ruled by princes or nobles, with titles such as archduke, duke, margrave, or count; others were bishoprics, where the bishop had both ecclesiastical and worldly authority. Some smaller territories were governed by the abbots of monasteries. There were also the free knights, who, in most cases, had no more than a castle and a domain of a few acres to govern and farm. Finally, there were the free cities. Some of these, like Augsburg and Nuremberg, owned large provinces, while others had only the small orchards and gardens around their walls.

All the German lands except Prussia, in the east, were within the boundaries of the Holy Roman Empire, as were the Netherlands, Switzerland, and Bohemia. This empire claimed to be the successor of the old Roman Empire. The Holy Roman Empire had been founded in the days of Charlemagne, who had ruled over a realm extending from northern Germany to southern Italy, and from the Atlantic to western Hungary.

Charlemagne marched into Italy to help the Pope against the rebellious Romans. After mass on Christmas Day, in the year 800, while Charlemagne knelt before St. Peter's Shrine in Rome, the Pope rewarded him by crowning him as Carolus Augustus, Emperor of the Romans. However, after the reign of Charlemagne, the Holy Roman Empire was never able to

The Holy Roman Empire in 1535

exercise its claim of imperial authority over all of Europe. The strife between church and crown, the bitter quarrels between successive emperors and popes, meant that no emperor was ever strong enough to secure either control over Italy for more than a short time or effective authority over all of Germany.

Moreover, the office of the Holy Roman emperor was not

hereditary but, rather, elective. When an emperor died, his successor was chosen by the seven most illustrious princes of the Empire, who were called electors. They were the arch-bishops of Mainz, Cologne, and Treves, the margrave of Bran-denburg, the duke of Saxony, the king of Bohemia, and the count palatine of the Rhine. For some years, however, it had been the practice for the electors to choose as emperor the head of the Hapsburg family, who ruled over the archduke-dom of Austria and other lands. The Hapsburgs wanted to establish the unquestioned authority of the emperor, but it was too late. In the past, the electors had taken care to appoint emperors who were unlikely to be strong rulers, and, as a re-sult, the Holy Roman Empire was now little more than a name. Outside of his own hereditary lands, the emperor had little power. There was no imperial army to enforce his will. The German princes were practically independent, and, if they did not choose to cooperate with the emperor, there was little he could do by himself. This situation—together with the fact that the current Holy Roman Emperor, Charles V, also ruled over important lands outside the Empire—was to be of great consequence for Luther and his followers in Ger-many. If the Holy Roman Empire had been like other Euro-pean states, if Charles V had not been a ruler with many other commitments, the fate of the Lutheran movement would probably have been very different.

Moreover, Lutheranism was shaped by the religious situ-ation in Germany as well as by political circumstances. In-deed, Luther's mission and message began as they did because of the condition of religion in Germany. His own religious progress was a struggle against the official religion of the time. The Church in Germany was part of the great Catholic Church organized throughout western Europe under the papacy. The pope was accepted and obeyed as the vicar of Christ—the representative of Christ on earth. Beneath him in every country were the bishops, ruling their dioceses and exercising authority over the many parish priests who administered the sacraments to the people. Only through these sacraments, it was believed, could men receive God's grace. In every country, there were also monks and nuns who lived in the cloister, apart from the world, and dedicated themselves to a life of prayer and meditation. In Germany, as in every European country, the Church was powerful and wealthy and claimed the allegiance of all the people so that they might gain their salvation in the life to come. The Church professed a high ideal that, for centuries, had dominated the life of all the European nations.

At the time of Luther's birth, the Church still outwardly maintained its prestige and its hold over the people. Its teachings were unquestioningly accepted, and the churches were well-attended. This was a religious age, though it was also a troubled one. Previous generations had known plague, war, famine, and other disasters, which had left their mark on the outlook of the people. They thought their sufferings were punishment for their sins. People believed that God and Christ were stern and angry judges, and many turned to the Virgin Mary and the saints to ask assistance in winning favors from heaven.

From childhood on, Luther was familiar with pictures that were painted on the walls inside German churches expressing this attitude. "They painted Christ," he later wrote, "sitting on a rainbow with His Mother and John the Baptist on either side as intercessors against His frightful wrath." For years, Luther was tortured by the idea of God's anger and stern justice, until he finally developed a new conception of Him.

People also believed that forgiveness of sins could be obtained by going on pilgrimages to pray at shrines containing the bodies or other relics of saints. Germany had one of the great European shrines—Cologne Cathedral, which drew pilgrims from many countries each year. The pilgrims came to visit its reputed tomb of the Magi, the wise men who visited the Christ child in Bethlehem.

Another German shrine was located at Wittenberg. There, the elector Frederick, Archduke of Saxony—who became Luther's protector—had assembled a large collection of relics in the Collegiate Church of All Saints, which was commonly known as the Castle Church. These relics included many remarkable acquisitions Frederick had obtained on a special journey to Jerusalem. The official catalogue of his relics, drawn up in 1509, listed 5,005 items, including 204 corpses of the innocent children slain by Herod, a piece of the burning bush seen by Moses, a part of the cradle of Jesus, and 33 fragments of the Holy Cross. Possessing these astonishing relics, Wittenberg took its place, as the Elector had hoped it would, among Germany's most popular attractions for pilgrims.

Despite the outward splendor and the popularity of the religious observances, all was far from well with the Church. It was, in fact, approaching a most serious crisis. The Church was, indeed, wealthy and strong, but, for a century and more, clergymen of all ranks and many religious orders had become more worldly and corrupt, ineffective, and uninspiring. The popes themselves had largely ceased to be spiritual leaders; they were now little more than Italian princelings, determined to increase their power, prestige, and territory. It was said that there were monks and parish priests who lived lazy, luxurious lives. As a result, there were people who now began to question the spiritual claims of the Church, and others who were envious of its wealth and resentful of its power.

In Germany, conditions were such that the state of the Church was worse and the resentment against it keener than elsewhere. The kings of France, Spain, and other countries had been able to limit the power of the Church in their kingdoms, but there was no strong central government to do this in Germany. Thus, the papacy was able to impose heavy taxes on the clergy and the people and to use German bishoprics to provide salaries for Italians who were at the papal court in Rome. In Germany itself, the princely bishops and abbots, who not only possessed large estates but ruled territories that amounted to about a fifth of the country, were particularly unpopular. The strongest hostility to the Church was felt by the middle-class citizens of the towns, who had grown wealthy through the development of trade and industry. They were jealous of the property and position of the clergy and regarded ecclesiastical power and privilege as remnants of an out-of-date feudal overlordship.

Yet, this was not the gravest criticism suffered by the Church. Its increasing failure to meet the religious needs of pious people everywhere was even more serious. Many of the pious no longer found satisfaction in the pilgrimages and other observances; they could take little part in church worship, because the services were still conducted in Latin. In his later years, Luther recalled the days when he had been a choirboy in the parish church: "A passage of the gospel was read aloud [in Latin], then the mass, but the people did not grasp the meaning of a single word." These plain, religious people were most deeply shocked by the failure of the priests and monks to live up to the ideals of their calling.

There had already been two reformers, John Wycliffe (*ca.* 1325–84), in England, and Johannes Huss (*ca.* 1369–1415), in Bohemia. Wycliffe and Huss both had wanted to restore the Church to its former state of humility and simplicity and to make Christianity the religion of the common people, instead of the preserve of the clergy. There were also mystics, in Germany and the Netherlands, who sought to establish a direct union between the soul of the individual believer and God through prayer and contemplation rather than through the rituals of the church.

One of these mystics was Meister Eckhart (*ca.* 1260–1327), a Dominican friar, who held that it was futile to search for God in the settled forms and services of the Church. Anyone was mistaken, he asserted, "who fondly imagines to get more of God in thoughts, prayers, pious offices, and so forth, than by the fireside or in the stall," but rather, he insisted, "The best and noblest way in which thou mayest come into this work and life is by keeping silence and letting God work and speak. . . . When we simply keep ourselves receptive, we are more perfect than when at work."

Though the mystics accepted the teachings of the Church, they implied that membership in it was not necessary for a man to know God and do his will. The mystics were a small group of devout men, but many ordinary German men and women also were seeking a personal religion of their own. Consequently, Luther's Germany was a country extraordinarily concerned with religion. People wanted to worship God in their own language and to study His message for themselves. They were no longer prepared to accept unquestioningly the Church as the supreme authority in spiritual matters.

In addition to the religious revival of these times, the countries of western Europe also were experiencing a great intellectual revival, which in many ways threatened the teachings and influence of the Church. This great rebirth of art and thought was the Renaissance. The Renaissance owed much to a revival of interest in ancient Greek and Roman civilizations, which had been neglected for centuries. In the early days of the Renaissance, people once again began to read the works of the great Greek and Roman philosophers, poets, dramatists, historians, and scientists. Once again, people studied and enjoyed the works of Greek and Roman painters, sculptors, and architects. The renewed study of these ancient cultures had a profound influence on the world of the Renaissance, particularly on life in Italy.

The Renaissance began in Italy in the fifteenth century and was encouraged by the popes, several of whom were munificent patrons of scholars and artists. Indeed, the Renaissance flourished in Italy, but it was not accompanied there by a revival of spiritual or moral life. Instead, its influence soon led to a decline in standards of conduct and to a renewal of crimes and vices that Christianity had long condemned. Even the papacy was not exempt from this tendency; the most brilliant period of the Italian Renaissance was also the time when the popes made the heaviest financial demands upon the people, exerted great political pressure, and were guilty of their most scandalous moral corruption.

When the new ideas of the Renaissance spread to Germany and the rest of northern Europe, they were welcomed by many educated men. But there were others in the northern lands who felt alien to the southern temperament of the Italian Renaissance and were deeply shocked by its irreligious and immoral character. This was one of the reasons why the Reformation, the movement that sought to reform the beliefs and practices of the Church, began in northern Europe. However, this spirit of reform was not united and led to many conflicting responses.

Among the men concerned with religious reform was the great leader of the northern Renaissance, the Dutch scholar Desiderius Erasmus (1466–1536). His study of the Greek version of the New Testament and his condemnation of the ignorance and laziness of priests and monks both had a strong effect in Germany. Erasmus wanted to see the extension of learning, which the Renaissance was accomplishing, together with the moral reformation of the Church, but he was not a revolutionary and feared extremes. His attitude toward Luther and his movement was, therefore, ambiguous. He wanted a reformation—but not the Reformation as it actually took place in Germany at Luther's instigation.

Most Germans, however, thought otherwise. Luther's passionate protests and vehement declarations, which, because of the invention of printing, were brought to them in books and pamphlets, aroused their immediate and enthusiastic support. Luther expressed their hopes and fears, resentments and aspirations. He was not only a truly religious man; he was also a great popular religious leader. He had a quick sympathy with the average man, a capacity to understand what the times demanded, and the ability to express it forcibly. He became the leader of a movement which had momentous and lasting consequences in Germany and throughout the western world.

2

Schoolboy and Student

Martin Luther was born on November 10, 1483, in Eisleben, a small town at the edge of the Thuringian Forest, in southwest Saxony. The baby was baptized the next day in St. Andrew's Church; according to the custom of the time, he was named after the saint commemorated on that day, St. Martin of Tours.

For generations the Luther family had owned a small farm near the village of Mohra in the western part of the Thuringian Forest. But Martin's father, Hans Luther, who, as a younger son, did not stand to inherit the farm, left the cottage soon after he married. Hans and his young wife Margaret moved to nearby Eisleben, where he found work in the newly-opened copper mines.

Hans Luther was an ambitious man, and when Martin was six months old, he and his family moved several miles away

from Eisleben, to the mining town of Mansfeld, which was in
the center of the copper industry. Life was a hard struggle for
the Luthers during those first years. Martin later recalled those
grim days. "When I was a small child," he said, "my parents
worked very hard. My father, as a young man, was a miner
and very poor. My mother gathered firewood in the forest
and carried home on her back all that was needed for the
household."

Within six or seven years, however, the Luthers' fortunes
had improved. The policy of the counts of Mansfeld, to build
and lease out small smelting furnaces, enabled thrifty and
skilled workmen to rise in the world. Hans had borrowed
money to lease several mines and furnaces, and soon he also
owned the house in which the family lived. He became a self-
made member of the middle class, a respected citizen of Mansfeld, and was chosen to sit on the town council. His family
grew to four boys and four girls, though in 1505 two of the
children died of the plague.

Martin Luther inherited a strong physique from his parents,
with whom he also shared a natural shrewdness, an impulsive
and violent nature, and an occasional crudeness of language.
His parents also gave him his early religious training. Both his
father and mother were devout Roman Catholics, who prayed
in the evening at their children's bedside. For them, Christian
beliefs were mingled with bits of old German paganism, which
had been handed down over the centuries from their peasant
ancestors. Devils and evil spirits, witches and goblins were viv-
idly real to them and to their children. Luther remembered
how his poor mother "was so tormented by one of her neigh-
bours who was a witch that she was obliged to treat her with
the highest respect and conciliate her, for she caused such
agony to her children that they would scream like unto

death." All his life Luther continued to believe in a personal, powerful devil who was ever-ready to assail and tempt good Christians.

Hans and Margaret Luther raised their children strictly and punished them severely. This was usual in the families of those days, and German parents had a reputation for being particularly stern and ready to beat their sons and daughters. A British traveler noticed that in most German homes a rod or a cane hung on the wall of the living room as a warning to the children, who were commonly made to take it down themselves before receiving their punishment. Martin later wrote of two particular instances of the discipline in his home: "My father once whipped me so that I ran away," and, "My mother caned me for stealing a nut, until the blood came." Yet, he always

Portraits of Luther's father and mother

considered that they "meant heartily well by me." He also recalled affectionately how his mother used to sing a little
rhyme:

> If people don't like you and me,
> The fault with us is like to be.

Hans Luther was ambitious for his son Martin; he wanted
him to be a lawyer and attain wealth and distinction. At the
age of seven, therefore, Martin was sent to school in his home-
town of Mansfeld. His schoolmates were other boys whose
parents hoped to send them later to the university to train for
the legal or clerical professions. The main purpose of such a
school was to teach its pupils Latin, the language essential for a
career both in law and in the Church. The boys had to learn
not only how to read and write Latin but also to speak it, and
the older boys were required to speak only Latin in school and
on the playground. One member of their class, called a *lupus*
or wolf, was appointed to keep a list of any of his fellow students who had spoken German.

Punishment was as common in the school as in the home.
Every noon the worst scholar in each class, known as the
asinus, was given a donkey-mask which he had to wear for the
rest of the day. For minor offences, boys were punished by
being hit on the palm of the outstretched hand with a ferula, a
flat piece of wood like a ruler which widened into a circle at
one end, where sometimes a hole was made to raise blisters on
the boys' hands. The ultimate punishment was a severe whip-
ping with the birch rod. It was the practice in many schools, at
the end of the week, that all the boys who had done poor
work, misbehaved, or spoken German were called up before
the class and beaten. If a boy had been found guilty of several
misdemeanors during the week, he was likely to get a dozen or

more strokes with the rod. It seems that Martin was treated as harshly by his schoolmasters as he was by his parents—"In a single morning, I received fifteen strokes with the birch rod for nothing at all. I was required to decline and conjugate and hadn't learnt my lesson."

Many years later, Luther criticized his schoolmasters for having given too much punishment and too little encouragement. With their harshness, he thought, they had smothered the love of learning in many of their students. Yet, he also had happy memories of his school days. He had good friends among the pupils, and, while he was still a small boy, some of the older students used to carry him on their back each day during the winter when the paths were deep in mud. Fifty years later, he gave one of them a Bible in which he had written, "To my dear old friend, Nicolas Oemler, who often carried me, a schoolboy, on his back to and from school, neither of us dreaming that one brother-in-law was carrying another."

During his school days in Mansfeld, Luther also enjoyed singing in St. George's Church, which stood across the square from the school. The boys of the school formed the church choir and had to learn by heart the *Te Deum, Benedictus, Nunc Dimittis,* and other Latin chants that were part of the services. These chants appealed to Martin's poetical temperament and love of music. He particularly liked the *Magnificat;* some twenty-five years later he was to translate it into German so that church congregations could understand and sing it.

On Easter Day in 1496, when he was thirteen years old, Luther's parents sent him away from home to a boarding school at Magdeburg. This school was conducted by the Brothers of the Common Life, an order established in the

Netherlands and devoted to the encouragement of personal religion among the people. Magdeburg was about thirty miles to the north of Mansfeld, in the broad valley of the great Elbe River. With a population of about 30,000, it was the largest city of the region and a flourishing member of the Hanseatic League. The city was also the seat of an archbishopric; it hád a massive cathedral and many churches, monasteries, and convents. In Magdeburg, Martin Luther had his first taste of the busy life in a great town.

It was here also that he first gained some knowledge of the monastic life. The order of his teachers, the Brothers of the Common Life, had been founded under the influence of the mystical movement. The Brothers were devout men who disliked the popular religious superstitions of their time and devoted themselves to the study of the Scriptures, to teaching, and to the performance of good deeds. The great Dutch scholar Erasmus also had been educated at one of their schools, which were noted for the care and training boys received there. The Brothers must have made a strong impression on Luther, for many years later he spoke of them as witnesses of Christian freedom and the apostolic way of life.

Another memory which he retained was his glimpse of Prince William of the reigning house of Anhalt, who had joined a Franciscan friary in Magdeburg, twenty-three years before Luther came to the town. Luther met him walking through the streets carrying a sack into which he begged people to place food for his friary. Thirty-five years afterward Luther wrote:

> Once when on my way to school at Magdeburg at the time when I was fourteen, I saw the prince of Anhalt going barefoot and cowled in the public street, begging for bread and carrying the sack like a donkey. He looked the image of death,

nothing but skin and bone; in fact, he died shortly afterward, unable to stand such a rigorous life. Those who saw him were struck with awe and could not help being ashamed that they too were not friars.

Luther spent only a year in Magdeburg. Then his parents sent him to another boarding school, St. George's School in Eisenach, which was some fifty miles southwest of Mansfeld, on the fringe of the hilly, rough country of the Thuringian Forest. Luther spoke later of "the dear old town of Eisenach," for he enjoyed his years at the school there. He admired the headmaster, the scholarly Johann Trebonius: "Every time he entered the classroom where his pupils were waiting, he took off his cap before he sat down in his chair. He made the other masters do the same, because, as he said, 'There is one or other of the young students whom God may make a worshipful mayor, a chancellor, a learned doctor, or even a ruler.' "

Eisenach was a much smaller town than Magdeburg. Most of its streets were unpaved, and its population was possibly even smaller than that of Eisleben, the little town where Luther was born. Yet, Eisenach was an important religious center, with many churches and monasteries within its walls. Later, when he was to dispute with many of the clergy, Luther would call Eisenach a "nest of priests"; but now his attitude was different. He became an admiring friend of the Franciscans, who had a friary at the foot of the steep hill on which stood Wartburg Castle—where Luther, many years later, was to be concealed for a time. In Eisenach, young Martin Luther became still more familiar with the life and work of the religious orders, especially with that of the Franciscan friars.

In 1501, in his eighteenth year, Luther left the school in Eisenach; but his education was not finished. His father had been prosperous enough to send him to boarding school and now could afford to send him on to the university. Hans Luther still wanted Martin to become a lawyer. He believed he could get his son a good position through the influence of the counts of Mansfeld. With this goal in view, he sent Martin to the University of Erfurt.

Erfurt, a city about the size of Magdeburg, was the capital of Thuringia. The city was surrounded by fertile fields, orchards, and vineyards, and stood on one of the great trade routes running north and south through central Germany. Erfurt had long been a flourishing town. It had fine churches and grand buildings—"Erfurt, city of towers," Luther called it. The university had been founded over a century before and was one of the best in Germany, particularly for the study of law. Over 300 new students came to it every year.

The students lived in colleges or hostels, which were conducted very much like monasteries, and they had to swear to obey the head of their college in all matters. Their day began with morning prayers in the college chapel and ended with evening prayers at eight, after which they had to retire to bed. They slept in dormitories and studied in a common room under the supervision of a tutor, who saw that they got on with their work and spoke only Latin. At the university, they attended lectures and exercises which began at six in the morning in the summer and at seven in the winter, and continued until the evening, with only an hour for dinner at midday. Once a week the students engaged in a disputation or class debate. They had to wear cap and gown in the college, at lectures, and in the streets. Students who broke university or college rules were usually fined, and in the colleges too, as in the minor schools, the rod was used to punish serious breaches of discipline or persistent failure to work; even twenty-year-old students were publicly whipped in the common room.

Though rules were strict, the students also had their pleasures and amusements. Some of the colleges brewed their own beer for lecturers and students alike. Luther's college, the College of St. George, may have been one of these, for it was nicknamed the "beer-bag." The students played games and had wrestling matches, and sometimes groups of students fought each other. There were also "town and gown rows," fights between townspeople and students. Several years after Luther had received his degree from Erfurt, one of these fights produced the "terrible year" of 1510, when a tavern brawl between students and workmen, who were assisted by mercenary soldiers, grew into a regular battle, which led to an attack on the university buildings and to the destruction of part of its valuable library.

Very little is known about Luther's student life at Erfurt. There is no record of his having done either anything distinguished or reprehensible there. Occasionally, he traveled home to Mansfeld on foot, walking the distance of fifty miles in three or four days. On one occasion, when walking back to Erfurt, he accidentally cut his leg on his sword; he was still half a mile from his college and reached it with great difficulty. He had lost a great deal of blood and was laid up for several weeks, during which time he taught himself to play the lute. Luther loved music, and he liked to sing songs with his friends. He later wrote that he first saw a complete Bible in the university library at Erfurt and was so interested that he spent much time reading it.

At Erfurt, Luther first had to study the three subjects known as the trivium—language, logic, and philosophy—in order to become a bachelor of arts. He received this degree in 1502, which was as early as he could; but his position in the class was only thirtieth out of fifty-seven. He then went on to

study the quadrivium—geometry, arithmetic, music, and as-
tronomy—which was the required course for the degree of
master of arts. He again completed his work as soon as possible
—in January, 1505. This time he was second among seventeen
candidates. The next month he received the master's brown
hat and delivered his master's address. Long afterward he remembered that day and its ceremonies: "Oh, what majesty
and splendor there was when the degrees were granted to the
new masters! They carried torches before them and presented
them. I think no earthly joy could be compared with it." Luther's father was delighted and proud and began to use the
formal *"Ihr"* instead of the intimate *"Du"* when he spoke to
his son.

Hans Luther was indeed pleased when Martin decided to
stay on at the university to read law at the College of St.
Mary, which stood near Erfurt's Cathedral. He could now expect that his son, after two more years of study, would be a
qualified lawyer with a good chance of securing a respectable
position as a counsellor to a prince or a town council. He also
had an eye on a rich wife for his Martin. Yet, while Hans
Luther was confidently making these plans, they were suddenly shattered.

Late in June, 1505, Martin once again walked home to
Mansfeld. After a few days with his family, he started his
journey back to Erfurt. It was a sultry July afternoon. In an
open field near the little village of Stotternheim, he was overtaken by a violent thunderstorm. There was a sudden bright
flash of lightning and a loud peal of thunder so close to him
that he flung himself to the ground. In his mortal fear, he
promised to join a religious order if God would spare his life,
and he called on the patron saint of the miners whose name he

must often have heard in his childhood days. "Dear St. Anne," he cried, "I will join an order."

Luther firmly believed that his experience was a summons, a revelation from God which he could not ignore. It was as real to him as St. Paul's conversion on the road to Damascus nearly fifteen hundred years earlier.

Martin's friends at the university were surprised and shocked when they learned of his intention, and they did their best to dissuade him. His father was bitterly disappointed and enraged that this son, on whose education he had spent so much money even before he had become prosperous, should deliberately flout his wishes and, as a result, would later not be in a position to support his parents in their old age. Luther, however, remained unmoved in his resolve. Like most men and women who had joined religious orders in the Middle Ages and in his own time, he believed that he must do so to save his soul; how could he disobey the divine summons? He was now twenty-two years old and had a strong mind of his own.

Within two weeks' time, he had arranged his affairs and decided what order he would seek to join. His friends gave him a farewell feast; afterward, they walked with him to Erfurt's Augustinian priory which he had chosen to join. There they stood and watched their friend Martin disappear as the heavy gate at the priory lodge closed behind him. Both he and his friends expected that he would spend the rest of his life serving God and earning salvation as a member of this religious order.

3

The Troubled Friar

During his student days, Luther had become especially well-acquainted with several orders of friars. These were men who followed the same life of prayer, worship, and meditation as monks; but instead of staying always within the walls of a monastery, the friars went out into the world to undertake such tasks as preaching, teaching, or charitable work. So, among the eight monasteric houses in Erfurt in 1505, Luther chose to go to the priory of the Augustinian friars, which was a flourishing and important house with a reputation for theological learning. It had some seventy friars, who taught at the university and preached in the city's churches. The Augustinian Order had been founded in 1243 and now had about 2,000 monasteries, which were located in several countries. Its priory at Erfurt was one of the order's thirty German houses, most of which were in Saxony. The Vicar General in charge of the Saxon province of the Augustinians was Johann von

Staupitz, a shrewd man of keen scholarship and deep spiritual perception, who, in time, was to become Luther's loyal, helpful friend.

In accordance with the Augustinian rule, Luther first had to spend a few weeks in the priory guesthouse, so that the prior could see whether he was in earnest and "whether his spirit was given by God." After he had passed this test, Luther was formally admitted into the priory chapel early in September, 1505, to serve as a novice for a year. The tonsure was shorn on his head, and he was clad in an Augustinian friar's black cowl and hood and the white scapular, a strip of material that hung from the shoulders down to the feet, as an emblem of the yoke of Christ.

Luther now entered a hard, disciplined life. He had a small cell, six feet by nine, sparsely furnished and unheated throughout the long, bitter winter. In this cell he slept and studied, leaving it to receive instruction on the Augustinian rule in the lecture room, to take his meals in silence with the rest of the community in the refectory, and to join the friars in the chapel for the seven services, contained in a book called the breviary, which they sang and recited in the course of each day.

As a novice, Luther was free to withdraw at any time, and the prior was equally entitled to decide that he was not suited for monastic life; but Luther came through the year of his noviciate successfully and took the irrevocable vows of poverty, obedience, and chastity which made him a friar. He now had to continue his studies and prepare for the priesthood. He was ordained and celebrated his first mass in February, 1507. Now he had completed the period of preparation and training, which had begun when he entered the priory eighteen months before.

Luther as a friar

Luther was a zealous friar. He was always ready to undertake the most menial tasks—to clean out the priory drains or to help in the kitchen. He willingly carried the begging-sack through the streets to get food for the community. He fasted, prayed, and flagellated himself in a manner which soon won him the reputation of a saint among his fellow friars. "I was a good friar," he recalled in 1533, "and kept strictly to my order; I could say that if the monastic life could get a man to heaven, I should have entered."

He also studied industriously and gained an equal reputation as a scholar, which led to his appointment to a teaching post and his move to another priory and university. Frederick of Saxony had founded a university six years earlier at Wittenberg, the small country town where he resided. Saxony, at that time, was divided into two states, an archdukedom and a dukedom. Frederick ruled the archdukedom, his nephew George, the dukedom. Duke George's capital was the great city of Leipzig, which had a flourishing university. Frederick wished to increase the reputation of both Wittenberg and his archdukedom and hoped to accomplish this through his collection of relics,* and his newly-founded university, though it had only a total of 150 students.

Frederick liked to have Augustinian friars as teachers at his university; they were good scholars and had to be paid only a small salary. Prior Staupitz had been appointed Professor of Theology, and it was probably through his influence that Luther joined him as a lecturer in October, 1508. So Luther moved from Erfurt to the Augustinian priory at Wittenberg, which Frederick was enlarging as part of his plans for the university.

Luther worked hard in Wittenberg, and though he would

* See p. 10.

Wittenberg in the sixteenth century

leave it for short spans of time, he was to spend most of his time there. He took classes in theology and continued his own studies. In 1512, the university made him a doctor of theology. That year Staupitz retired from his professorship and obtained the appointment of Luther as his successor.

Over the next six years Luther, now a professor of theology, gave a series of lectures on the Psalms and another on the Epistles of St. Paul. He usually lectured twice a week from six to seven o'clock in the morning and sometimes also from noon to one o'clock. When Erasmus published his edition of the Greek version of the New Testament in 1516, Luther at once learned Greek and used it for his lectures. When he explained the Scriptures, Luther shared with Renaissance scholars a concern with the literal truth of the text, and he was not content with the interpretation placed upon it by the medieval Church.

A young Augustinian friar from Cologne, who attended Luther's lectures on the Epistle to the Galatians in 1517, gave this portrait of him:

> He was a man of middling height, with a voice both sharp and gentle; it was soft in tone, sharp in the enunciation of syllables,

words, and sentences. He spoke neither too rapidly nor too slowly, but evenly and without hesitation, very clearly, and so logically that each part flowed naturally out of what went before. He did not get lost in a maze of language, but first explained the individual words, then the sentences, so that one could see how the content of the exposition arose and flowed out of the text itself. For it all hung together in order; word, matter, natural and moral philosophy. . . . There never was anything in his lectures that was not relevant and full of meaning.

In addition to his professorial duties, Luther was busy in many other ways. His ability, industry, and religious inspiration, together with the powers of leadership he was beginning to show, had gained him the confidence of the authorities of his order, who soon heaped numerous tasks upon him. In October, 1516, he wrote to a friend in Erfurt:

I require two scribes or secretaries. I spend almost all my time writing letters, so that I am not sure whether I am repeating what I have said before. I am lecturer at the friary and reader during meals. I am also called from day to day to preach in the parish church, act as regent of studies at the priory, and I am subvicar which means prior of eleven friaries, have to gather the fish at Leitzkau, administer the affairs of Herzberg at Torgau, lecture on Paul, edit my lecture on the Psalms—and besides am burdened with writing letters which, as I have said, takes up much the greater part of my time. I don't have enough time for the prayers in the breviary or for saying mass. In addition to all that, I have to fight the temptations of the world, the flesh, and the devil. You can see how much leisure I have.

Amid all this work and responsibility, however, Luther was sadly troubled in his mind and conscience. In another letter, written that same year, he said, "My life draws nearer and nearer to hell. Day by day I become worse and more wretched." When he was a devout and serious young man, he had become a friar to save his soul. He believed that God had called him to this way of life and that through it God would use him for His purpose.

Yet, as the years went by, Luther could find no spiritual satisfaction in the religious observances of the order, however hard he tried to execute them. "Who knows," he once asked himself, after several days of exhausting services and penances in the priory, "whether these things please God?" Though his zeal and perseverance in performing his tasks gained him the admiration of the other members of his community, he was increasingly haunted by the fear that this way of life brought him no nearer to God, no nearer to salvation. "I was trying to cure the doubts and scruples of the conscience with human remedies, the traditions of men," he said later. "The more I tried these remedies, the more troubled and uneasy my conscience grew."

As a religious man, Luther was constantly and urgently plagued by the contrast between the supreme goodness of God and the desperate wickedness of man. "It is God's eternity, holiness, and power which thus continuously threaten men throughout the whole of his life," he wrote. "God's ever-present judgment grasps hold of man in the loneliness of his conscience, and with his every breath conveys him to the Almighty and Holy One to prosper or be destroyed." Luther feared God's judgment. He was overwhelmed by a sense of his own wickedness. He believed that he was among the worst of sinners. He found himself in a state of despair before God. He longed to be reconciled to Him and to be assured of His forgiveness, but he could find no assurance that this ever could be. Although he confessed his sins and did penance for them, as the rules of the Church required, he still felt himself to be an unredeemed sinner, condemned by God's inexorable justice.

Most of Luther's superiors and companions at the priory grew tired of his constant anxieties. If he remained a faithful friar and accepted the means of salvation offered by the Church and the order, they assured him, he need have no doubt that his soul would be saved. Some of them tried to comfort him and to restore his peace of mind by assuring him that he was a good servant of God and had not committed any serious sins; but they could not relieve his anguish. Luther believed that he was wholly sinful because his heart was disobedient to the will of God, and he did not know how to come to Him. Really, no one could help Luther; he had to find his own way.

While he was experiencing these grave personal perplexities, Luther was also becoming more and more dissatisfied with the condition of the Church, as he knew it. His studies of ecclesiastical history had made him see a glaring contrast between the life of the early Church and the Church of his own day. He was particularly critical of those priests who were paid solely to say masses in order to save the souls of the dead who were believed to be in purgatory, the intermediate condition between heaven and hell. He roundly condemned "those foolish and impious churchmen who swagger about with the gifts which they have received from the laity and think they are doing their job when they mutter a few prayers on behalf of their benefactors."

Earlier, in 1510, when Luther was still studying for the doctorate and when his doubts were beginning to plague him, he was sent, with another friar, to Rome to represent the order on a matter of business. The two friars went there along one of the pilgrim routes through Switzerland and northern Italy and spent four weeks in the city. To Luther, Rome was still the seat of the Vicar of Christ and the center of Christendom. When he first saw the city in the distance, he knelt down on the road and said, "Blessed art thou, Holy Rome!"

Luther took no interest in the new St. Peter's Basilica and the other great buildings and monuments of the Renaissance. He visited the catacombs and the shrines where pilgrims were accustomed to pray. One of these was the Scala Sancta, the twenty-eight steps close to the Lateran Church, which, it was claimed, were the very steps, once located in front of the Jerusalem courthouse, from which Pontius Pilate had shown Christ to the mob. Pilgrims now crawled up the Scala Sancta on hands and knees, repeating the Lord's Prayer at each step, in the belief that this act would release a soul from purgatory. Luther did this on behalf of his grandfather—"but when I got to the top I thought, who knows if it is true?"

Luther returned from Rome, not only disturbed by such doubts but also shocked by the scandalous tales he had heard about some of the Renaissance popes, and by evidence he had seen of the immorality, laziness, and irreverence of the Roman clergy.

Luther was made a professor at Wittenberg soon after his return from Rome.* He was soon again immersed in teaching at the university and in his many other activities. He also returned to his unrewarded search for the grace of God. He had sought grace through the services and sacraments, the practices and ceremonies of the Church; but he felt they had failed to bring him the desperately yearned-for assurance that he

* See p. 30.

was accepted and forgiven by God. Several more years of anxiety and uncertainty were still before him, but he now began to take the course that was to bring him the peace and certainty he had so long and earnestly desired.

Prior Staupitz, who had always been ready to help and advise Luther, persuaded him to read the writings of the German mystics.* Luther was especially attracted by the books of Johannes Tauler (*ca.* 1300–61), a Dominican friar who had been a disciple of Meister Eckhart. Tauler emphasized God's compassion and the love of Christ for man as He had shown it on the Cross. He also taught that all souls who truly seek to know and serve God must pass through a period of great suffering but must persevere in their efforts until they attain peace of mind and a perfect understanding of Him. "Life does not consist in repose," Tauler said in a sermon, "but in progress from good to better." Through the work of preparing his university lectures, Luther came to a deep understanding of the Scriptures, especially of the Epistles of St. Paul, who insisted that the spirit of Christ had made him free from the burden of the law. Luther's studies helped and reassured him in the conclusions he was beginning to form about the personal and inward nature of true religion.

As with his decision to become a friar, Luther's final discovery of spiritual peace and relief from anguish came to him suddenly. One day, in 1515, while he was studying St. Paul's Epistle to the Romans in the reading room of the priory tower, he thought again—as he had been doing for weeks—about the seventeenth verse of the first chapter, "The just shall live by faith." Suddenly he sprang up from his chair with joy, because the meaning had become clear to him, and with it the solution to his troubles. In the last year of his life, he still

* See p. 12.

remembered this experience so clearly that he could write fully about it:

> I greatly longed to understand Paul's Epistle to the Romans and nothing stood in the way but that one expression, "the justice of God," because I took it to mean that justice whereby God is just and deals justly in punishing the unjust. My situation was that, although an impeccable friar, I stood before God as a sinner troubled in conscience, and I had no confidence that my merit would appease Him. Therefore I did not love a just and angry God, but rather hated Him and murmured against Him. Yet, I clung to dear Paul and had a great yearning to know what he meant.
>
> Night and day I pondered until I saw the connection between the justice of God and that statement that "the just shall live by faith." Then I grasped that the justice of God is that righteousness by which, through grace and sheer mercy, God justifies us through faith. This immediately made me feel as if I had been born again and had entered paradise through newly-opened doors. The whole of the Scriptures took on a new meaning, and it became to me inexpressibly sweet in greater love, so that the passage of Paul became to me a gate of heaven.
>
> If you have a true faith that Christ is your Saviour, then at once you have a gracious God, for faith leads you in and opens up God's heart and will, that you should see pure grace and overflowing love. Thus it is to behold God in faith that you should look upon His fatherly, friendly heart, in which there is no anger nor ungraciousness. He who sees God as angry does see Him rightly, but looks only on a curtain, as if a dark cloud had been drawn across his faith.

4

The Question of Indulgences

To Luther, the Pauline text, "the just shall live by faith," was a promise that seemed to provide, at last, the answer to his problems. Now he believed that no one could earn salvation by his own works—not by the prayers, fasting, and penances with which he had so earnestly occupied himself. Instead, he had now come to believe that God freely grants forgiveness of sin and eternal life to all who earnestly repent, believe in the message of the Gospel, and have faith in Him through Jesus Christ. Once a man puts his trust in God and discovers His grace, Luther now reasoned further, he is justified through faith. The human heart, he felt, is too wicked to save itself; forgiveness is God's gift, which cannot be earned by personal efforts. This was Luther's doctrine of "justification by faith alone"; it was to become the watchword of the Reformation.

Luther's views soon became apparent in his university lectures, which attracted large and eager audiences. Among those

who heard his lectures on the Epistle to the Romans was Philip
Melanchthon (1497–1560), who was appointed professor of
Greek at Wittenberg in 1518 and became Luther's faithful
supporter. Melanchthon said of him:

> He made these writings so clear that the light of new learning
> seemed to arise after a long and dark night. Here he distin-
> guished between the Law and the Gospel, here he refuted the
> error which then reigned in the schools and assemblies, which
> teaches that men merit remission of sins by their own works,
> and that men are justified with God by discipline as the Pharisees
> taught. . . . All devout people were much taken with the
> sweetness of his doctrine, and it was welcome to the learned,
> as though Christ appeared from darkness, prison, and filthiness.

Luther always denied that his ideas were new. He had
found them by studying St. Paul's Epistles, and he showed
that St. Augustine also had put them forward in his writings.
Nevertheless, they had long been overshadowed by other
teachings. Luther's proclamation of them now had revolutionary implications; it seemed to threaten the whole position of
the medieval Church.

Over the centuries, the Church had developed a system de-
signed to enable men, through participation in its sacraments
and observances, to gain the salvation of their souls. But if men
could only be saved by turning directly to God to receive His
grace, then the whole system of the medieval Church was ren-
dered useless and even harmful. The clergy, then, were no
longer the vital mediators between men and God, and the sacraments were no longer absolutely necessary channels of divine grace. All these, according to Luther's ideas, were re-
placed by the need for a personal relationship between God
and each individual Christian, for faith was the means by
which he would receive the supreme gift of grace.

During these years, however, Luther was not accused of heresy when he put forward his views. On the contrary, he gained the support first of Wittenberg's theological teachers and then of the university as a whole. Although he was critical of the abuses in the Church, he regarded himself as its loyal member and, indeed, had not consciously revolted against it. Before long, however, an event occurred which was to transform him from an unknown university teacher into a figure known throughout Germany and in many countries beyond its borders.

The Renaissance papacy was on the verge of bankruptcy. None of the popes ever had an annual income half as great as that of the republic of Venice, but in their dual position as princes and ecclesiastics their expenditures were far greater. Lavish patronage of great artists and architects, and attempts to establish the prestige of the papacy in European politics added to their financial difficulties. One pope, Innocent VIII, was compelled to pawn his tiara in 1484. In such financial stress, successive popes made desperate and determined efforts to add to their income by increasing the fees, dispensations, exemptions, and other legal payments from bishops and other churchmen. The church sought to raise money from lay people on a large scale. The offerings of the many pilgrims who came to Rome were considerable, and indulgences proved to be consistently profitable.

There had been a theory behind the practice of indulgences in the medieval Church: After a penitent sinner had made private confession to a priest, he was absolved from the eternal punishment meted out for every mortal sin. But still, the sinner had to undergo punishment to pay for his sin, either in this life or in purgatory. It was believed, however, that the pope could grant indulgences, which would enable men to escape doing penance for their sins, be it penance in this life or the pains of purgatory in the next. People believed that indulgences could be granted, because the saints, who had performed works of piety and virtue in excess of what was required for their own salvation, had bequeathed to the church an inexhaustible "treasury of merit," which could be transferred to needful sinners.

Indulgences had been granted to those who took part in the Crusades; in 1300, Pope Boniface VIII had proclaimed a year of jubilee and granted full pardon to all who made the pilgrimage to Rome that year. This had been so profitable to the papacy that indulgences were offered on an increasing scale. The next important development came in 1476, when Pope Sixtus IV offered indulgences for the redemption of souls in purgatory, to be purchased by their friends and relatives on earth. Indulgences were now granted to those who contributed a sum of money to a pious purpose, and, in 1510, Pope Julius II promised indulgences to those willing to contribute to the rebuilding of St. Peter's Basilica in Rome. Thus, indulgences had become a regular means of raising money for the papacy; but inevitably, indulgences had led to gross abuses.

It was a particular abuse of indulgences that aroused Luther to act upon his beliefs. In 1517, Pope Leo X commissioned Archbishop Albert of Mainz to proclaim, throughout Germany, the indulgence on behalf of St. Peter's and allowed him to keep half of the proceeds for his archbishopric. Albert needed money badly, because he was heavily in debt to the banking house of the Fuggers. With the money he had borrowed, he had paid for the papal dispensations that enabled him to hold three bishoprics at once. In order to get as large a profit from the indulgences as possible, Albert appointed as his chief agent, Johann Tetzel, an eloquent and unscrupulous Dominican friar.

Tetzel visited town after town in Germany. As he ap-

A portrait of Tetzel, with his hand on his money box and with indulgences, marked with different prices, neatly arranged above him

proached the city walls, the members of the town council met him and escorted him in a solemn procession down the main street amid waving flags and pealing church bells. In front of him was carried a cross bearing the papal arms and the papal bull (or document) setting out the indulgences, which rested on a gold-embroidered velvet cushion. The cross was set up in the market place, and Tetzel spoke to the people. He required no evidence of repentance for their sins from those who bought an indulgence for themselves, and he also proclaimed that anyone buying one for a dead relative could obtain the immediate release of his soul from purgatory. In his harangues, he represented the unhappy souls in purgatory as loudly beseeching their relatives and friends to purchase an indulgence and relieve them from torment. His words were satirized by a contemporary rhyme:

> As soon as money in the coffer rings,
> The soul from purgatory's fire springs.

Tetzel could not sell indulgences in Wittenberg. Archduke Frederick did not permit him to enter Saxony, for the Archduke was afraid that the counterattraction of the friar's campaign might reduce the number of pilgrims visiting his own relics. The papacy had attached important indulgences to Frederick's relics; it has been estimated that they carried with them a possible total remission of 127,799 years and 116 days from purgatory. But Friar Tetzel was offering a complete and immediate release. Owing to the broken territorial line of Saxony, however, Tetzel could come near most parts of Frederick's land without actually crossing the borders, and a number of people went from Wittenberg and its district to obtain his indulgences.

To Luther, indulgences now seemed to be a particularly flagrant example of the wrongful ideas about the forgiveness of sins upheld by the Church. He thought Tetzel's mission was a blasphemous swindle, which would lower the standards of Christian life and blind men to the true way of finding God's salvation. When people returned to Wittenberg with the pieces of paper they had bought from Tetzel, he was indignant, and in October, 1517, he nailed to the door of Wittenberg's Castle Church a list of ninety-five theses or arguments, written in Latin, against indulgences and pilgrimages.

This was not a revolutionary act of defiance on his part. It was, and had long been, a common way for a scholar to announce that he wanted to debate some matter with other scholars. No one came to debate with Luther, and it looked at first as if his pronouncements would have no more effect than those of many other scholars before him.

If Luther had lived a century or so earlier, this almost certainly would have been the case. He himself made no attempt to spread his Theses among the people, but others, who sympathized with his ideas, soon began to do this. They surreptitiously translated them into German and had them printed on the presses which had been established in the country during the preceding seventy years. In this way, Luther's words were spread quickly throughout Germany, and they were widely read. Although he had written his Theses for academic debate, his style was bold, uncompromising, and easily understood, and the "Ninety-five Theses" made a deep impression on those who read them.

Many Germans had long felt that their country was being robbed by the papacy. They were now roused by Luther's Theses which attacked Pope Leo X's use of indulgences to rebuild St. Peter's. "The revenues of all Christendom are being sucked into this insatiable basilica," wrote Luther. "The Germans laugh at calling this the common treasure of Christendom. Before long all the churches, palaces, walls, and bridges of Rome will be built of our money."

Such statements were not new. Complaints about the greed of popes had been made for many years. But in his "Ninety-five Theses" Luther also based his opposition to indulgences on spiritual grounds:

> Indulgences are most pernicious because they introduce complacency and thereby imperil salvation. Those persons are damned who think that letters of indulgence make them certain of salvation. . . . Peace comes in the word of Christ through faith. He who does not have this is lost even though he be absolved a million times by the pope, and he who does have it may not wish to be released from purgatory, for true contrition seeks penalty. Christians should be encouraged to bear the cross. He who is baptized into Christ must be as a sheep for the slaughter. The merits of Christ are vastly more powerful when they bring crosses than when they bring remissions.

Few people responded to this call to crucify the self and follow Christ; but among those who did were the nation's religious leaders, who were to inspire the spiritual revolution that followed Luther's action at Wittenberg.

In the unexpected excitement which was aroused by the publication of the "Ninety-five Theses," Luther had the support of his fellow friars and teachers at Wittenberg and also that of the Saxon Elector. Frederick seemed less concerned about the criticism of his relics than about the academic renown of his university, whose most distinguished professor was Luther. Archbishop Albert was alarmed. In several towns, Tetzel was so violently threatened by mobs that he had to withdraw hastily, and his sales of indulgences decreased considerably. The Archbishop decided to refer the matter directly to the Pope, rather than enter into an open dispute with Frederick of Saxony and the Augustinian Order.

Pope Leo X thought that this matter was rather a trivial affair and instructed the Augustinian authorities to keep their members under better discipline. Luther answered a summons to justify himself before them in Heidelberg in April, 1518, and defended his views so ably that he converted many of his superiors. As support for Luther in Germany continued to grow, Leo reluctantly realized that he had to act. In August, he summoned Luther to Rome, but Luther did not comply with this summons directly. Instead, he appealed for protection to Frederick, who secured him a hearing at Augsburg before Cardinal Cajetan, a great Dominican theologian. Cajetan was not willing to argue with Luther about indulgences. He told him, "You have only a word of six letters to pronounce, and the whole business will be dropped: *Revoco* (I recant)." He wished to make Luther realize that persistence in his attitude would lead him into the very dangerous position of opposing the pope's authority; but Luther replied that the truth was better than any alternative. In the end, Cardinal Cajetan said, "I shall not talk to that creature again for he has deep eyes and marvelous speculative ideas in his head."

Leo X had meanwhile issued a papal bull upholding indulgences; but he had no wish to become embroiled in German affairs. He now sent an envoy, the Saxon nobleman Carl von Miltitz, who was a papal chamberlain, with instructions either to induce Luther to retract or to persuade Frederick to surrender him to papal authority. The papal envoy failed in both attempts. As an observant diplomat, he noticed how strongly German opinion was on Luther's side. He was impressed by Luther when he met him in January, 1519. "Martin," he said, "I imagined you were some aged theologian mumbling argu-

ments to himself in a cozy corner behind the stove. I find you
are young and strong and original." The most he could do was
to persuade Luther to write to Pope Leo X, submitting to his
authority, but retracting nothing.

When the excitement over his "Ninety-five Theses" first
broke out in Germany, Luther was not pleased to discover
that he was regarded by many as the leader of an attack on the
papacy. "The song," he said, "was pitched in too high a key
for my voice." But his interviews with Cardinal Cajetan and
envoy Miltitz made him reconsider his attitude towards the
papacy, and during the spring of 1519, he studied its history.
He could find no support in Scripture for the claim that the
bishop of Rome had authority over all Christians and no evidence that the early Church had accepted this claim. Luther
believed that final authority must rest with a council of the
Church, a general assembly of bishops from all countries. Such
councils had met in the past, but their importance had dimin-
ished in the face of the growing power of the popes. Luther
now held that the pope must submit to the authority of a
council, which should meet as soon as possible.

His ideas became even more radical after he agreed to a
public disputation with Johann von Eck, a professor at Ingolstadt in Bavaria, who had bitterly criticized Luther. The debate took place in the Dukedom of Saxony, during the summer of 1519. It was held in the great hall of Duke George's
castle of Pleissenburg near Leipzig. Luther spoke from a lectern hung with a cloth embroidered with a portrait of St. Martin of Tours; Eck's lectern was decorated with an embroidered hanging that depicted St. George killing the dragon.

The discussion lasted ten days. Eck was a skillful debater
and soon forced Luther to assert that even a council of the
Church could err and that Scripture was the only authority.

Pope Leo X with two cardinals

There was turmoil in the hall when he made this statement, because Johannes Huss, who had been condemned as a heretic a hundred years earlier,* had held such a view. Yet, Luther was conservative in outlook. He assumed such an uncompromising position reluctantly, but having taken it, he stood firm. "We are all Hussites without knowing it," he later said in February, 1520. "St. Paul and St. Augustine are Hussites."

The disputation with Eck increased Luther's reputation. Many theological students came to Wittenberg (as the Elector had hoped they would); there were not enough rooms in the town to lodge them. The books Luther began to write sold well in Germany. He wished to make his position clear and to urge his beliefs upon the clergy, the rulers, and the people of his country. His language was sometimes violent and extreme because he had an ardent nature and felt keenly about what he wrote. "I am hot-blooded by temperament," he wrote in 1520, "and my pen gets irritated easily." The gentle Melanchthon once commented on his writings, saying, "The truth might fare better at a lower temperature." Yet Luther was a great writer. His style was direct, forceful, and clear. He could write disputations, devotional books, sermons, and hymns of equal excellence. His writings, despite their flaws, were to do much to shape the Reformation in Germany.

The most important of Luther's writings during the year 1520 were his *Three Treatises*. The first, *To the Christian Nobility of the German Nation*, called upon the German princes to reform the Church themselves, since the clergy had not done so. This was their duty because, Luther insisted, laymen have as important a part in the life of the Church as the clergy, who have no special privileges and have only been set

* See p. 12.

apart to perform certain functions. Luther was presenting another revolutionary doctrine, that of "the priesthood of all believers," which asserted that all Christians have an equal priestly calling in the Church. All Christians have their responsibilities toward God. The princes in particular, as rulers of the people, must care for both their subjects' material and spiritual welfare.

The second treatise, *On the Babylonian Captivity of the Church*, was an attack on the sacramental system of the Church. In this book, Luther declared that there were only two sacraments—Baptism and Communion. He now denied the validity of the other five sacraments recognized by the church—penance, confirmation, extreme unction, holy orders, and marriage. Moreover, he asserted that the sacraments were not means to salvation brought about by the action of the officiating priest; they were occasions on which the believer could receive grace through faith given him by God. It was this treatise which led Henry VIII of England to write his book against Luther's ideas.* Luther flatly replied to the King, "The gospel that I, Martin Luther, preach will conquer and overthrow pope, bishop, monks, kings, princes, devil, sin, and everything else not of Christ or not in Christ. No one can prevent it."

Luther's third treatise, *Of the Liberty of a Christian Man*, was, although short, perhaps his most important book; it contained the key to his spiritual position. It was based upon St. Paul's words in his First Epistle to the Corinthians: "I am a free man and own no master; but I have made myself every man's servant, to win over as many as possible." From this text, Luther drew two main ideas—"A Christian is by his faith

* See p. 3.

the free master of all things and subject to none," and "A Christian is by his love a humble servant in all respects and subject to all others." In the conclusion of the book he said:

> From faith flow love for God and delight in God, and, out of love, the free, unconstrained, happy life of service to our fellows. . . . A Christian lives, not in himself, but in Christ and his neighbors; in Christ by faith and in his neighbor by love. By faith he rises above himself unto God; from God he stoops below himself by love; and yet he remains always in God and in divine love.

Pope Leo X was at last alarmed by Luther's publications and decided to act. In June, 1520, he condemned Luther in the bull *Exsurge Domine*, so named because it began with a quotation from Psalm 68: "Let God arise, let his enemies be scattered . . . for foxes are about to lay waste Thy vineyard, which Thou didst entrust to Peter, Thy vicar. A wild boar from the woods is soon to ravage it." Pope Leo X preferred hunting wild boar to studying theology. Indeed, he was out on such an expedition when this very bull was brought to him to sign, which perhaps explains the introductory quotation. This bull condemned Luther's views, ordered his books to be burned, and gave him two months to recant or else be treated as a heretic.

Eck, who had written much of this bull, was foolishly given the task of publishing it in the Holy Roman Empire. He took it to the young Emperor Charles V at Antwerp, and he obtained his permission to publicly burn Luther's books in the market places of the leading towns. The burnings took place without incident in the Flemish towns of Louvain and Liège, but in the German university towns, the students resolutely opposed Eck. At Cologne and Mainz, they rescued Luther's books from the fire and threw anti-Lutheran books into the flames instead. At Leipzig, they stoned Eck and forced him to take refuge in a Dominican friary. He did not dare to go to Wittenberg, but he did try to enter Erfurt, only to be opposed by a group of armed students from Luther's old university. It was almost impossible for him to execute the bull anywhere.

During the controversy of the past three years, Luther's confidence had been increasing, and he showed this by his resolve to reply to Eck in kind. Early one December morning, a crowd of students and townspeople gathered, in answer to his summons, just outside Wittenberg's Elser Gate at the place where it was customary to burn the clothes of those who had died of the plague. Here a bonfire was made, into which were cast, symbolically, volumes of ecclesiastical law. Then Luther himself, amid shouts of jubilation, flung into the flames the papal bull which had condemned him, declaring, "Because you have condemned the truth of God, He also condemns you today to the fire. Amen."

As the paper blazed and the smoke rose high into the sky, the crowd sang the *Te Deum*. Later in the day, the students arranged their own celebration. To the sound of music and revelry, they paraded around the town with another copy of the bull affixed to a pole and an indulgence on the point of a sword.

5

The Diet of Worms

The day after the burning of the papal bull Luther addressed his audience of some 400 students in German, before beginning his lecture in Latin. "You too," he said, "must choose for yourselves between hell and martyrdom. If you do not take the field against the papal anti-Christ, you will be faced with the question of eternal damnation. But if you decide to take the field, you must be prepared for martyrdom."

Luther had traveled a long way since, as a young friar, he first began to have doubts about the Church's system of salvation. He had not begun as a rebel; but his desire to be reconciled with God and his dissatisfaction with the Church had led him, step by step, to challenge doctrines it had upheld in Europe for centuries. Similarly, when he first protested against indulgences, he had merely thought that Pope Leo X had allowed the practice because he was mistaken and ill-informed, but now he believed that the papacy itself was anti-Christian, and that those who supported it were endangering their souls. Moreover, the question no longer was a doctrinal dispute between theologians. It had become a popular topic, and Luther's attitude was steadily gaining more support among the people. Around Wittenberg, peasants were stopping travelers on the road to question them—"Are you for Martin?"—and beat them up if they were not.

Despite such popular support, however, Luther had good reason to suppose that he and his supporters might face martyrdom. Huss and many of his followers had been burned at the stake as heretics. In January, 1521, the Pope put Luther's excommunication into effect by another bull, *Decet Pontificem Romanum*. It was now the duty of the imperial authorities to arrest Luther and hand him over to an ecclesiastical court for trial, but Luther was still under Frederick's protection. The great question was, therefore, what Emperor Charles V would do.

Charles had been Holy Roman Emperor for just over a year. He was a young man of twenty, but the rule of vast territory was concentrated in his hands. From his father he had acquired the Burgundian lands of Franche Comté, Luxembourg, and the Netherlands; from his maternal grandparents he had inherited Sicily, Naples, and Spain with its vast territories overseas. And upon the death of his paternal Hapsburg grandfather, Emperor Maximilian, he had been elected Holy Roman Emperor and had also inherited the Hapsburg family lands.*

It was natural that Charles should wish to link his great and scattered dominions in Europe into one huge, united empire; but another young monarch, King Francis I of France, was determined to resist him. In fact, for much of his reign Charles

* See p. 8.

was at war with Francis, and, at the same time, he was forced
to protect his eastern territories against Turkish attacks.
Charles, like previous emperors, would have liked to increase
his power in Germany; but the German princes would never
submit to this. The new religious movement now rapidly
growing up around Luther presented Charles with his greatest
single problem; but his attempts to deal with it were crippled
by his many other commitments, concerns, and frustrations.

In religious matters, Charles was conventionally devout and
regarded the Church with uncritical veneration. His imperial
office made him the protector and defender of the Church and
its faith, and he was cautiously conservative in his attitude toward religious reform. He realized that there were matters in
the Church that needed mending, but he did not believe that
low standards of duty among some of the popes and other
similar abuses affected the validity of the Church as a divine
institution. To Charles, the spectacle of a friar challenging the
authority and traditions of the Church was immodest and dis-
tasteful.

Emperor Charles was now in Germany. In October, 1520,
he had gone to Aachen to be crowned Emperor in the cathedral where Charlemagne lay buried, and in January, 1521, the
young emperor convened a meeting of the Imperial Diet, an
assembly of the princes and the representatives from the free
cities of Germany, at the historic town of Worms on the
Rhine. This Diet was to decide what to do with Luther. Since
he had been excommunicated, the ecclesiastical authorities
urged the Diet to take action against him. Charles wanted this
to be done, but a number of the German princes sympathized
with Luther, and a stormy debate ensued. Eventually, it was
decided to invite Luther to come to Worms and appear before
the Diet. Though Charles gave him a promise of safe-conduct,

Emperor Charles V

it required courage for Luther to go. Huss had gone to the
Council of Constance in 1415 under a similar safe-conduct
promise, only to be burned as a heretic. Yet, Luther immediately accepted the invitation. "Though there were as many
devils as the tiles on the roofs, I should be there," he declared.

He set out for Worms with three companions in April,
1521, as soon as the Easter festival was over. His university
gave him a sum of money toward his expenses, and the town
council of Wittenberg provided him with a two-wheeled cart
for his journey. He spent a weekend in Erfurt. He preached
that Sunday in the familiar Augustinian priory chapel, which
was so crowded that the beams of the gallery began to creak
in such an ominous fashion that the congregation began to
panic, until Luther calmed them by saying that it was the devil
trying to trick them into fear. After a two-week journey
through the Saxon lands and then up the broad valley of the
Rhine, he and his companions came within sight of Worms.

The last stage of their journey was like a triumphal procession. A number of eminent people, most of them from the
court of Frederick of Saxony, went out several miles on horseback and on foot to welcome them and escort them into the
city. The guard at the gate, seeing the approach of such an
imposing company, announced their coming with a blast of
trumpets. Although it was lunch time, the streets were
thronged with cheering people, who pressed against the walls
of the houses as Luther's little cart rumbled along to the lodgings in the house of the Knights of St. John, which had been
found for him in the crowded city. Here about 2,000 people
saw Luther alight, and some heard him remark, "*Deus erit pro
me*" (God will be for me).

Among those watching Luther's arrival in Worms was the

papal legate to the Diet, the scholarly Cardinal Aleadro, a Venetian, who noticed with chagrin how a priest actually bent forward to touch Luther's robe, as if he were a saint. Aleandro, indeed, became alarmed by Luther's popularity with the German people. He wrote, "Nine out of every ten cry, 'Luther,' and the tenth, 'Death to the Court of Rome.' " Only a few of Luther's followers understood his concept of justification by faith or the other theological points at issue; but the people knew that Luther had defied the pope and attacked the Church's claims to its power and its privileged position.

On the following day, at four o'clock in the afternoon, Luther was escorted by the imperial marshal to the bishop's palace, where the Diet was meeting. Again, the streets were crowded, and Luther was taken by a back road through a garden to the palace. He was led at once to the bishop's chamber, in which Emperor Charles and the Diet were assembled. The room was packed with people to the point of suffocation. One who saw Luther standing there saw him as "a man . . . of forty years of age, more or less, vigorous in expression and physique, eyes without distinction, mobile of countenance, and frivolously changing his expression. He wore the habit of the order of St. Augustine, with leather girdle, his tonsure large and recently shaven, his hair closely clipped." Charles V's immediate impression of Luther was not complimentary. "That man," he said shortly afterward, "will never make me a heretic."

Luther's books, collected by Cardinal Aleandro, had been piled on a nearby bench. In a letter written shortly after this meeting, Luther gave his account of it: "This afternoon I faced the Emperor and the papal legate, who asked me whether I wished to repudiate my books; and I must say tomorrow whether I repudiate them. I merely requested to be given a brief opportunity for consideration. If Christ grants me His blessing, I shall not recant a dot or a comma."

Luther appeared again before the Diet at six o'clock in the evening of the next day. This time, because of the discomfort experienced by everyone the day before, the meeting took place in the great hall of the bishop's palace. Even this great room was so full of people that Luther had difficulty in making his way to the stand. It was dark now, and the flaming torches, which illuminated the hall, added to the heat. At the previous meeting, Luther had seemed nervous and overawed by the great men who were facing him and had appeared to be uncertain about recanting. He had spent the night in great inward conflict, but by evening had regained his self-assurance. His courage now helped him rise to the occasion. After admitting that his attacks on the papacy had perhaps been too violent, he said, "I do not set myself up to be a saint." He then answered firmly to the question which had been put to him the day before and was now repeated. "Unless I am convicted by Scripture and plain reason (for I do not accept the authority of popes and councils, since they have often erred and contradicted each other), my conscience is captive to the Word of God. I cannot and I will not recant anything, for to go against conscience is neither right nor safe. God help me. Amen." It is not certain whether he actually concluded, saying, "Here I stand; I can do no other," since these words only appear in a later account of the proceedings of the Diet; but they certainly represent the unyielding stand he now took.

Luther's reply was heard in hushed silence. Then there was a moment's uproar before Emperor Charles brought the meeting to an end. Luther was sweating profusely from the heat in the overcrowded hall; but he was buoyant now that he had made his position clear. As he left the building, Charles V's Spanish troops, who were guarding the palace, scoffed at him. "To the flames!" they cried. But Luther and his friends ignored them and, to quote an observer, "raised their arms, moving hands and fingers, as the Germans do for a signal of victory at the tournament." When Luther reached his lodgings, he shouted to the crowd, "I've come through, I've come through!"

Luther thought, indeed, that his appearance before the Diet was an anticlimax and almost a waste of time. He wrote a jocular letter to his friend, the painter and engraver Lucas Cranach, saying, "I would have thought that His Imperial Majesty would have assembled fifty doctors to confute the friar in argument, but nothing of the sort. All that was said amounted to this: " 'Are these books yours?'—'Yes.' 'Do you recant?'—'No.' 'Then get out!' "

The walls of Worms were now plastered with posters for and against Luther. Emperor Charles wanted to take immediate action against him, but many of the princes were still opposed to this. Not until a month later was Charles able to issue the Edict of Worms, which put Luther under the ban of the empire, making him an outlaw and forbidding all to give him shelter or to read his writings. Meanwhile, for a week, a small committee composed of members of the Diet tried to reach a compromise with Luther, but they failed. "The pope," Luther declared, "is no judge of matters pertaining to God's word and faith; but a Christian man must examine and judge for himself." Luther was now told to leave Worms. His safe-conduct was renewed for twenty-one days.

Luther wrote a brief message to the Emperor and the Diet, assuring them of his loyalty and claiming that he wished only to reform the Church and to have freedom to bear witness to the word of God. The next morning, he and his companions set out for Wittenberg, accompanied by an imperial herald and armed guards, who were to see that he completed his journey as prescribed and then arrest him when the safe-conduct expired. The Emperor had sent him word that he was not to make speeches on the way; but Luther replied that it was scarcely possible not to say anything. He preached in the chapels of the monasteries where the party stayed overnight and also in the village church at Mohrs, where he was given a night's lodging in his grandmother's house.

This was the last sermon of the journey. Shortly after leaving this village, as Luther and his companions were driving through the Thuringian Forest, their wagon was halted by five armed horsemen. The driver shrieked with fear, and the guards fled as fast as they could. Luther's friends made a pretense of resistance, so that the driver would report that Luther had been overpowered by enemies; but this was a pre-arranged ruse known to Luther and his friends. Seizing his few books, he allowed himself to be placed by his captors on a horse and led over side roads for the rest of the day. At dusk, they neared Eisenach and toward midnight entered the gates of Wartburg Castle, which belonged to Frederick of Saxony.

The wise Frederick had decided that it was best and in Luther's own interest that he should be hidden for a time.

Rumors spread at Worms about Luther's fate. "Some say I captured him," wrote Aleandro. "Some say the Archbishop of Mainz. I wish it were true!" Other rumors had it that Luther's body had been found in a silver mine with a dagger plunged into it. When people questioned Frederick, he said he did not know where Luther was. Frederick had purposely left the execution of his plan to others and at first did not know where Luther had been taken.

Wartburg Castle

Luther, indeed, was very much alive. He was lodged in a chamber of the castle and waited upon by two pages. His identity was known only to the warden of the castle, who kept a close watch on him. To everyone else, he was "Sir George," and he dressed the part. He had discarded his friar's habit and dressed as a knight, with a gold chain round his neck and a sword at his side. He allowed his beard to grow and covered his tonsure with a small red cap.

After years of activity and controversy, Luther disliked the peaceful and quiet life in the castle. "Here I sit an odd captive," he wrote, "willing and yet unwilling—willing because God so wills it, unwilling because I should prefer to stand forth in behalf of the Word, but have not yet been found worthy." He slept badly, as the owls and bats wheeled about outside in the darkness, and when he did sleep, he had nightmares, often about the devil who came in the shape of a big black dog and lay on his bed until he threw him out of the window. To divert his hidden guest, the warden once included him in a hunting party; but Luther was revolted by the cruelty of the hunt. "There is some point," he reflected, "in tracking down bears, wolves, boars, and foxes; but why should one pursue a harmless creature like a rabbit?" One little rabbit took refuge in his sleeve, and to his disgust the dogs bit through the cloth and broke its neck.

Gradually, Luther's spirits returned. From the window of his room, high in Wartburg Castle, he looked across to the dark, wooded Thuringian hills from which arose here and there the blue columns of smoke coming from the kilns of the charcoal-burners. Then a gust of wind blew them away and cleared the sky, and Luther felt that God had dispelled his doubts and restored his faith. He stayed in Wartburg Castle through the summer and winter; then came the spring, which for Luther always had carried a message of hope. "Our Lord," he said, "has written the promise of the Resurrection, not in books alone, but also in every leaf of springtime."

Meanwhile, he had found relief from the irksomeness of captivity in study and writing. He alarmed the cautious warden by insisting on going to Eisenach to borrow books from the library of the Franciscan friary he had known as a schoolboy. He also insisted on writing to his friends. The warden feared he would betray his hiding place, but he headed his letters: "From the Isle of Patmos," or "From the Wilderness."

Above all, he began to translate the Bible into German. He completed the whole New Testament in just over a year, using the text of Erasmus, and then he began to work on the Old Testament. He was to finish his translation of the whole Bible by 1534, thirteen years later. Since for Luther the word of God was the foundation of religion, he was determined to make it readily available to the people. He said, "It [must] have its place in the hands, tongues, eyes, ears, and hearts of men." He took care to write simply and in the common language of "mothers in the house, children in the street, and men in the market place." Together with his hymns, this German Bible was to be a mighty force of the Lutheran Reformation.

6

Turmoil and Conflict

While Luther was in Wartburg Castle, the Edict of Worms was issued against him and his supporters, and Charles attempted to enforce it. In the Netherlands, he was able to take severe measures against Luther's followers, and two friars of the Augustinian priory in Antwerp were put to death as heretics. In Germany, however, the sympathizers of the new movement were so numerous that it was impossible to carry out the Edict. Indeed, although Luther was in hiding, his influence was as strong as ever. It has been estimated that by that time, about 300,000 copies of his books had been sold. "I perceive," the Emperor's secretary wrote, "that the minds of the Germans are generally exasperated against the Roman see, and they do not seem to attach great importance to the Emperor's edicts, for, since their publication, Lutheran books are sold with impunity at every step and corner of the streets and in the market places."

The university at Wittenberg continued to flourish, and exciting events were taking place in the town. In Luther's absence, the leadership of the movement was taken over by three men—the scholarly and moderate Philip Melanchthon; Andreas Karlstadt, a much more radically minded professor; and Gabriel Zwilling, an Augustinian friar and something of a popular agitator. All three were eager to put Luther's teaching into practice. Melanchthon took the first step. Luther had said that the practice, adopted by the Church in the Middle Ages, of administering Communion in one kind—that is, giving the bread only and not the wine to the communicants—was wrong. Accordingly, on Michaelmas Day, in the fall of 1521, in the Parish Church, Melanchthon administered to a few students Communion of both kinds—that is, both the bread and the wine. This was an important change in the practice of worship, for it gave heed to Luther's insistence upon the equality in the Christian community of priests and lay people.

Melanchthon, however, found it increasingly difficult to restrain his two enthusiastic colleagues. They both wanted to take more extreme action than he thought wise. And they had many supporters in the university, the priory, and the town who were roused by their words. That year, on Christmas Eve, an excited mob, among whom were many students, rushed into the Parish Church, smashed lamps and images of saints, heckled the priests, and sang in the church an irreverent song, "My maid has lost her shoe." Then, from the courtyard, they heckled the choir. They went on to the Castle Church, and, as the priest there was giving the blessing, they wished him pestilence and hell-fire. On Christmas Day, a congregation of nearly 2,000 was in the Castle Church (although the total population of Wittenberg was only about 2,500), and Karlstadt, in a plain black gown instead of vestments, recited the mass for them in Latin, but he omitted the passages designating the mass a re–enactment of Christ's sacrifice as well as the elevation of the elements at the consecration—not lifting bread and wine for the congregation to see and adore. He then invited the people, in German, to take the bread and wine from the altar with their own hands.*

Early in 1522, the town council of Wittenberg approved these changes in the mass and ordered all the side altars and pictures of the saints to be removed from the Parish Church to avoid "idolatry." The town council also took over a number of funds that pious benefactors had set up in the past to pay priests to say masses for the dead. The council placed these funds under the control of a committee of laymen, who were to use them for the maintenance of the parish clergy, the relief of the needy, and the provision of dowries to enable poor girls to marry. At the same time, the town council forbade monks and friars to beg and ordered them to support themselves by work. Luther's fellow friars at the Augustinian priory showed themselves in favor of the new developments. Under Zwilling's leadership, they destroyed the side altars in their priory chapel, burned the pictures of the saints, and smashed the images.

These changes, though moderate compared with what was to happen later in other places, seemed too extreme to the elector Frederick. He was alarmed by the violence and rioting, particularly when neighbouring princes and bishops began to complain to him. Frederick was now in poor health and anxious not to provoke strife. However, he was unwilling to disown Luther and his colleagues, whose religious sincerity and academic ability he admired. He urged caution on the town council, which was placed in a quandary. It had no wish to

* See p. 81.

quarrel with its ruler and patron, but it was determined that there should be religious reform in the city.

The situation in Wittenberg also worried the conservative-minded Luther. He feared that the disorder and disunity would spread. He was horrified when he received at Wartburg Castle a message from Karlstadt asking his opinion about the marriage of monks. Luther had himself declared a year ago that it was lawful for priests to marry, since it was in accordance with the outlook of the New Testament and the practice of the early Church, but the training and teaching he had received in his youth still made him feel embarrassed by the idea of monks or friars marrying. "Good God! Our Wittenbergers will give wives even to the monks!" he declared. "But they will not thrust a wife on me!" Yet, when he came to consider the question, he found that he had to give it his approval. He wrote a pamphlet, *On Religious Vows*, in which he asserted that the monastic life was not a special calling for Christians, but rather that the Gospel had to be practiced in the world and that there was no higher calling than a man's everyday work, which he should perform to the best of his ability.

His words were soon acted upon in Wittenberg. Karlstadt had already married before he received Luther's reply. Others quickly followed his example. The friars at the Augustinian priory held a meeting at which they decided that all members who wished to renounce their vows were free to do so. Fifteen friars immediately left the priory, and others followed until, within a few months, the prior was its only occupant. Many of the former friars married, some of them choosing former nuns, which shocked many of the more conservative people. Monasticism had been the most important part of medieval Christian society, and this step was the beginning of its dissolution in several European countries.

By Easter of 1522, the situation in Wittenberg seemed dangerous. The extremists had enthusiastically welcomed the arrival of three self-styled "prophets" from Zwickau, a city near the Bohemian border, who claimed to have received direct from God visions that would have made the Bible unnecessary. Melanchthon said frankly, "The dam has broken, and I cannot stem the waters." The alarmed town council decided to ask Luther to come back and restore order. Luther, despite Frederick's fears for his safety, decided to return. He had already made a brief visit to Wittenberg shortly before Christmas. Now he set out on horseback from Wartburg Castle to resume his permanent residence in Wittenberg. Melanchthon looked up in surprise when a knight who had a thick black beard and was clad in a scarlet cloak and woolen tights stepped into his room, but Luther soon donned his Augustinian habit, shaved, and prepared to recover his religious leadership in the town.

Luther went up again into the pulpit of the Parish Church, from which he had been absent for over a year. He urged moderation upon his followers:

> What you did was good, but you have gone too fast, for there are brothers and sisters on the other side who belong to us and must still be won. . . . Faith never yields, but love is guided according as to how our neighbours can grasp or follow it. There are some who can run, others who must walk, and still others who can hardly creep. Therefore we must not look on our own, but on our brother's powers, so that he that is weak in faith . . . may not be destroyed. . . . Let us therefore throw ourselves at one another's feet, join hands, and help one another.

People would think, he said, from Karlstadt's foolish preaching, that a man was a Christian if he communicated in both kinds, did not go to confession, and smashed images—"Behold the malice of Satan, how he has tried in a new way to compass the ruin of the Gospel!"

Luther secured his objective in eight sermons. The people of Wittenberg deserted Karlstadt. Zwilling agreed not to celebrate mass wearing a round, flat cap with a feather in it. He left the town to take charge of a nearby village church, and, soon afterward, Karlstadt did the same. Reform now took place, under Luther's leadership, by persuasion and consent rather than by violence and intimidation. In March, 1523, Luther began to introduce his reformed services in the Parish Church. As a friar, he had been wearied by the long, drawn-out repetition of the daily round of monastic services, so he insisted that no services should last longer than an hour. He also wanted the preaching of the Bible to have a prominent part in every Sunday service including the mass. He abolished the celebration of saints' days, except those in honor of the Virgin Mary. He remolded the actual service of the mass, introducing German hymns and providing for Communion in both kinds; he also made changes in the other services, translating them into German and refashioning them so that the people could take part in them.*

Though Luther urged moderation, he strongly criticized the Dean and canons of the Castle Church for holding fast to the old order and singing masses for the souls of the dead. Townspeople smashed the windows of the canons' houses and made life so uncomfortable for them that at last the Dean wrote to the Elector saying that they could no longer fulfill their duties there. The new services were then introduced in the Castle Church. About the same time as the canons gave up control of their church, the Augustinian prior vacated the fri-

* See p. 81.

A contemporary portrait of Luther the reformer

ary buildings, which, together with the garden, the Elector now presented to Luther as his own residence. Here he lived for the rest of his life, making his home a busy center of missionary activity.

While Luther was restraining the religious tumults at Wittenberg, there were other outbreaks of violence in Germany. In 1522, the knights, once important but now reduced to insignificance and poverty by the growth of trade and the rise of the princes, rose in rebellion but were defeated within a year by a princely army. There followed, however, a more serious revolt in the German countryside.

As merchants and businessmen had become more prosperous, the great German landowners wanted to increase their income from their estates. To do this, princes and noblemen, bishops and abbots began to increase the amount of work and other obligations exacted from their peasant serfs. This inflamed feelings of anger and discontent that had long been harbored by the peasants. At the same time, the peasants were encouraged by Luther's attacks on the abuses and claims of the Church. Their resentment was given violent expression in the fiery sermons of wandering preachers with radical views, like Thomas Münzer, who called upon the people in the villages to rise against the nobility and clergy and seize their lands. "On while the fire is hot," he cried, "Let not your swords be cold from blood!" Münzer had been a follower of Luther but now thought that Luther was too moderate and conservative, and he called him "Dr. Easychair and Dr. Pussyfoot," "Brother Soft Life," and "Dr. Liar."

The Peasants' Revolt began with a series of isolated uprisings in southwestern Germany in 1524. One of these broke out in June of that year because of demands made by the Countess of Lupfen on her estates at Stühlingen, northwest of the Black Forest. The Countess insisted that her serfs were to collect strawberries and snail shells (on which she would wind her silks), when they wanted to gather the harvest on their own land. By the spring of 1525, the trouble had spread to many parts of southern and central Germany. Castles, manor houses, and monasteries were sacked and set on fire, and their occupants were slaughtered.

Because he was himself the son of peasants, Luther sympathized with the rebels and believed that many of their grievances were justified. When the risings began, he wrote:

> It should plainly be understood that, from the very first, a wise prince has been a rare phenomenon and a devout one still rarer. As a rule, they are the greatest blockheads and the worst rogues on earth. . . . They can hardly do anything else than flay and beat [peasants] and add one burden upon another. Now God is going to punish them by the rebellion of the oppressed, who

An attack on a monastery during the Peasants' Revolt

ought not, cannot, will not endure your tyranny and insolence any longer. No longer is the world in such a state that you can please yourself how you drive and hunt human beings. Therefore, let the Word of God do its work.

However, as the violence and bloodshed increased, Luther's attitude changed. The peasants had distorted his plea—that men should possess their spiritual rights—into a demand for political and social rights. He told them, "If you are anxious to appeal to the rights laid down by the Gospel, then remember that these rights consist in suffering with Christ on the Cross." He had never meant his teaching to produce revolt and bloodshed. People were already calling the peasants "Lutherans," and, if it were thought that he supported them, all religious reform would be impossible. After the authorities had suppressed the Peasants' Revolt, they would suppress his movement as a threat to law and order. He risked his life by traveling around the country to preach against violence.

Appalled by news of a massacre at Weinsberg in which, to the sound of pipes, the peasants had speared the Count of Helfenstein and his retainers in the presence of his wife and child, Luther wrote his most intemperate pamphlet, *Against the Murdering, Thieving Hordes of the Peasants,* saying:

If the peasant is in open rebellion, then he is outside the law of God, for rebellion is not simply murder, but it is like a great fire which attacks and lays waste a whole land. Thus, rebellion brings with it a land full of murders and bloodshed, makes widows and orphans, and turns everything upside down like a great disaster. Therefore, let everyone who can, [stop those who] smite, slay, and stab, secretly or openly, remembering that nothing can be more poisonous, hurtful, or devilish than a rebel. It is just as when [one] must kill a mad dog; if you don't strike, he will strike you and the whole land with you.

When Luther wrote those words, the Peasants' Revolt was at its height and seemed likely to plunge all Germany into civil war; but the electors of Saxony and Hesse and the Duke of Brunswick quickly united to raise an army, and, in May, 1525, they overwhelmed a large force of peasants at Frankenhausen. Soon the revolt had been put down everywhere. Thousands of peasants were slain or hanged. Luther had been carried away by his temperament and his vocabulary, and, when his tract had appeared, it had seemed like a call to the princes to show no mercy to the defeated rebels.

It is difficult to say how much support Luther lost because of his condemnation of the Peasants' Revolt. Certainly, many of the poorer classes now turned to the new revolutionary sects called the Anabaptists, which spread in Germany and neighboring countries. But the Anabaptists were almost destroyed through persecution by governments that feared their attacks on privilege and property. Nevertheless, many Germans had been terrified by the Peasants' Revolt, and Luther won strong support from the upper and middle classes, who were educated enough to appreciate the need for religious reform, disliked the power of the papacy, and wanted to limit the rights and wealth of the Church. It was with their powerful assistance that Lutheranism now made progress in Germany. Without them, it could not have defied both pope and emperor.

It was, indeed, all the more important for Luther to have the sympathy of these important classes in Germany since, about this time, he lost, to his deep sorrow, the support of Erasmus and other scholars, including Luther's friend Staupitz. Erasmus was seventeen years older than Luther. At first, he had praised Luther because he "had attacked the crown of the pope and the bellies of the monks," but later he said, "I laid

Erasmus

a hen's egg; Luther hatched a bird of quite a different breed."
Erasmus wanted the Church reformed, its abuses abolished,
and the primitive faith of the early Christians revived. He did
not criticize the Church's teachings, sacraments, or form of
government. He was opposed to controversy and argument—
"I am averse to any action which might lead to commotion
and uproar"—and also to any reform that would destroy the
unity of the Church. This was the real point of difference between the two reformers. Luther believed that Christian truth
and the salvation of men's souls were of such importance that
they must be pursued above all else and at whatever cost.

7

The Lutheran Church

In May, 1525, the Archduke Frederick of Saxony, who had given Luther such valuable protection, died. Frederick was succeeded by his brother John, a man who was even more favorably inclined to Luther's cause. In John's dominions, Luther now took a step he had hardly anticipated when he had made his first protest against papal policy: He organized a Lutheran church, which was entirely separate from the old Roman Catholic Church under papal supremacy. Originally, Luther had hoped that the emperor would summon a council to reform the whole Church; but since Charles was an ally of the papacy, this would not be done. Luther now believed that it was right that the Church should be reformed wherever possible in Germany, despite pope and emperor. And so Lutheranism began to spread beyond Wittenberg and Saxony, into many parts of the country.

The general popularity of Lutheranism was demonstrated

by the people of the free cities, who were the first to revolt against the papacy and to reform the churches within their walls. This reformation began to take place in the 1520's. By 1524, Nuremberg, the most powerful of Germany's free cities, had put Luther's ideas into practice. Its example was soon imitated by Strasburg, Ulm, Augsburg, and many smaller southern cities. Between 1528 and 1531, the most important northern cities, among them Hamburg, Bremen, and Magdeburg, did the same. Before very long, about two-thirds of the free cities had gone over to the Reformation. Of the larger cities, only Regensburg (which was dominated by the conservative dukes of Bavaria) and Cologne (which was restrained by its Archbishop) remained consistently loyal to the papacy. In cities which became Lutheran, the Reformation was carried out by the town council or the craft guilds, which dissolved the monasteries, reformed church worship, and brought new, Lutheran clergymen into the churches.

After the free cities, some of the larger German states, ruled by princes, began to adopt the Reformation. Albrecht of Hohenzollern, Grand Master of the Teutonic Knights, a military order which governed East Prussia, was the first to make such a move. In 1525, he dissolved the order, took possession of its lands, became a Lutheran, and declared himself the first duke of Prussia. His action caused a sensation. Soon, several German rulers followed his example and joined the Reformation. The landgrave of Hesse became a Lutheran in 1526; the margrave of Brandenburg-Ansbach, the dukes of Schleswig and Brunswick, and the counts of Mansfeld all became Lutherans in 1528. In these states, the rulers adopted the new faith and established it as the religion of their subjects; they made the necessary changes in religious organization, using Saxony as their model.

Now Lutheranism really spread in Germany, not as the result of a single great movement but in a piece-meal fashion, through a number of separate reformations, each of them organized by the city and state authorities who were able to attract to the new ideas the citizens within their jurisdiction.

Luther saw no reason why this should not be so. He had already declared that the princes were responsible for the religious well-being of their subjects.* He felt that it was consequently the duty of each ruler to reform the church in his domain. Moreover, Luther was dependent upon the princes and rulers of the land. If the Church were to be reformed in Germany, it had to be done by those who possessed power in the various cities and states.

This situation inevitably influenced the organization of the Lutheran church in Germany; it was very closely connected with the governing authorities. Whenever Luther went anywhere to assist in the church reformation, he always took with him one theologian and three lawyers. Reform required drastic changes in the law and, therefore, had to be accomplished through the direct cooperation and intervention of the magistrates of a city or the prince of a state. These governing authorities usually took possession of the monastic lands and other property of the old church and administered them for religious, education, and charitable purposes. The German rulers and city councils also transferred to themselves much of the old authority of the bishops.

A prince now would exercise the old jurisdiction of the bishop through a consistory, which was usually composed of lawyers and clergymen and was appointed by the prince. Sometimes the prince himself presided over its meetings, but more often he appointed a deputy. The consistory acted

* See p. 49.

mainly as an ecclesiastical court and exercised all disciplinary powers in the church. Parishes were grouped together into districts, each of which was under the supervision of a clergyman, who was given the title of "superintendent"; but only the consistory could appoint and remove a clergyman from his post and determine the details of the worship conducted in the churches.

In the beginning, these newly reformed states secured new, Lutheran pastors for their parishes, from the University of Wittenberg, where Luther continued to teach. As soon as possible, however, Lutheran princes arranged for their own universities to train candidates for the ministry, and some of them established new universities to do this. In Hesse, monastic buildings were given over in 1527 for the use of the new University of Marburg, which was the first university to be founded by Lutherans; others followed in the course of the century.* Luther himself had great influence on these universities. Some of their most important teaching posts went to men who had studied under him at Wittenberg, and they were determined to maintain the same high standards in theological learning he had set for them there.

An educated ministry was essential for the new church, because Luther stressed the importance of preaching. In the Parish Church at Wittenberg, three services were held every Sunday, and there was a sermon at each of them; there was also a sermon on every night of the week. Luther was assisted in this by a staff of clergymen, but he took a large share in it, sometimes preaching at all the services on a Sunday and four times during the following week. Luther believed that it was the continual duty of the preacher to explain and interpret for the people the Word of God. In It alone, he believed, was to be

* See p. 5.

found the truth which would help men in the trials and temptations of the world and bring them to eternal life. He insisted, therefore, that the sermon must have a prominent part in Christian worship so that every congregation would be instructed in their faith.

Luther also wanted the services in themselves to be a means of instruction. Though he did not agree with the changes made by Karlstadt in the mass at Wittenberg, he believed that the people should be able to understand the service and participate in it, and that there must be a mass in German. Luther's first German mass was held in 1526. This mass, however, was not just a translation from the old Latin service. Luther no longer accepted the medieval doctrine that each celebration of the mass re-enacted Christ's sacrifice on the Cross and that at each mass His body and blood were offered anew to intercede with God for man's sin. He followed Karlstadt, therefore, in omitting from his mass all reference to sacrifice as well as the elevation of the consecrated elements, held up high by the priest for the people to see and adore. He sought to restore the emphasis that the early Church placed on the service as an act of worship in which Christians united to praise God and strengthen their fellowship through Christ, with Him and with each other.

In many ways, however, Luther left the traditional forms of worship unaltered. The clergy were to wear the old mass vestments and continue much of the old ceremonial. There were still to be candles on the altar and a crucifix, which some wished to remove as idolatrous, but Luther said, "When I hear Christ speak, my heart forms the image of a man hanging on the Cross. Far from it being a sin, it is well that I have the image in my heart. Why then should it be a sin to have such a picture before my eyes?" In the churches themselves, the only

important change to take place was the disappearance of the
side altars, which had been placed there in the Middle Ages
because of the large number of masses said every day by the
priests. Luther wanted the people to communicate every time
they attended mass (instead of infrequently as hitherto) and
so he confined the celebrations to Sundays and holy days, ren-
dering the side altars useless.

Besides denying that the mass was a sacrifice, Luther could
not accept the medieval doctrine of transubstantiation, which
held that as the bread and the wine were consecrated, they
were inwardly changed into the body and blood of Christ,
although they remained bread and wine in outward appearance. He never quite clearly expressed what he believed to
happen at the consecration, but he always insisted that Christ
is really and truly present at every celebration. The stand that
he took on this point destroyed the chances for unity among
the forces on the side of the Reformation.

While Luther was bringing about his reform at Wittenberg,
other reformers were also taking action against the papacy and
the abuses of the Church. One was Ulrich Zwingli (1484–
1531), who, by 1525, had reformed the Church and its services in the important Swiss city of Zurich. Since the ideas and
goals of Luther and Zwingli seemed very similar, Philip of
Hesse, one of the first German princes to become a Lutheran,
wished to bring the two reformers together. He arranged a
meeting between then at his castle in Marburg, in 1529. They
reached agreement on a number of matters but found themselves utterly opposed on the issue and meaning of the sacra-
ment. Zwingli regarded the Communion service as essentially
a commemoration of Christ's sacrifice for mankind. He regarded the bread and wine as unchanged symbols of His body
and blood. Luther could not consent to this concept. He

A portrait by Holbein of Ulrich Zwingli

pulled back the heavy velvet cloth from the table at which they sat and chalked on it the Latin version of the words Jesus spoke at the Last Supper—"*Hoc est corpus meum*" (This is my body). He would not accept Zwingli's interpretation that these words were a symbolic figure of speech, meaning, "This signifies my body." After four days of discussion, this meeting in Marburg ended; the two men parted without having made the alliance Philip of Hesse had hoped for.

Philip was a young convert to Lutheranism, impetuous and continually active. He had been anxious to promote an understanding between Lutheranism and Zwinglianism in order to counter the attempts being made to check the progress of the Reformation in Germany and restore the whole country's allegiance to the Roman Catholic Church. At first, these attempts had not been successful; the princes had refused to enforce the Edict of Worms in their territories. Successive Diets had failed to reach any solution of the religious problem, and Emperor Charles V was too pre-occupied with his wars against France in Italy to make a serious attempt to suppress heresy throughout the Empire. By 1529, however, Charles was victorious in Italy; now he hoped to be able to act more effectively in Germany. Though he could not be present at the Diet of Speyer, which met that year, he demanded that action be taken. The Diet ordered the enforcement of the Edict of Worms and forbade princes to seize more Church lands. A number of princes and free cities replied to this with a printed "Protestation," in which they affirmed their right to answer to God alone for what concerned "God's honor and the salvation . . . of the souls of each one of us," and insisted "they must protest and testify publicly before God that they could consent to nothing contrary to his Word." From this time on, because of this official document, the "Protestation," all who opposed the papacy came to be known as Protestants.

In 1530, Charles at last returned to Germany; his purpose was to attend the Diet of Augsburg. The meeting of the Diet was preceded by a great service in Augsburg Cathedral, but when the Emperor and the congregation knelt to receive the Archbishop's blessing, the Protestant princes remained standing. Charles was scandalized when he heard that these princes were attending Lutheran sermons in the city. He summoned them to his presence and demanded that they should no longer do this. "Sir," said the old Margrave of Brandenburg-Ansbach, "rather than that I would leave off the Word of God, I will kneel here on the spot and lose my head." Charles was so taken aback that he could only stutter in broken German (his native language was Flemish), "My dear lord, no heads off."

Since Luther was still formally under the imperial ban, which had been imposed by the Diet of Worms, he was not able to go to Augsburg. But as he wished to be at hand, he stayed for six months in the Castle of Coburg. Again it was spring-time, and, as in the spring when he was hidden in Wartburg Castle, he was inspired. On the wall of his room he inscribed a text in Latin taken from Psalm 118, "I shall not die, but live and proclaim the works of the Lord." This was the psalm that pleased him most. "My own, my chosen psalm," he called it; and, in this, reformer and emperor were for once of one mind, for Charles V said it was "my own special favorite."

King Charles V had come to Augsburg with the intention of securing religious unity in Germany. He had hoped to get a council summoned which might agree to the reforms the Lutherans wanted; but the popes who had succeeded Leo X were austere, religious men, very different from the earlier Renaissance popes, and determined to make no concessions to heresy.

Charles, therefore, decided to attempt reconciliation himself. He asked the Protestant princes to state their position. The result was the Confession of Augsburg, drawn up by Melanchthon, who tried to be as conciliatory as possible. He omitted such controversial topics as purgatory and transubstantiation, stressed justification by faith, but said nothing of the priesthood of all believers.

The Augsburg Confession was a moderate statement of Lutheran beliefs, and Melanchthon concluded, "This is almost the sum of our teaching. It can be seen that nothing in it is discordant with the Scripture or the teaching of the Catholic Church or the Roman Church as it is known from ancient writers. We are therefore judged unfairly if we are held to be heretics. Our disagreement is over some abuses which have crept into churches without due authority."

Luther was uneasy about the Confession of Augsburg, fearing that in its desire to be conciliatory it had blurred disagreements and obscured the truth; but openly he praised it and expressed his hope that it would succeed: "I have been through our friend Philip's *apologia*," he wrote, "and it seems to me quite excellent. I should be at a loss to know how to alter or improve it. Nor should I be willing to try, because it is impossible for me to speak so gently or cautiously. May Christ our Lord grant that it will bear much rich fruit, as we all hope and pray. Amen."

The peace move, however, failed. The papal legate, Cardinal Campeggio, insisted that the Lutherans must accept full papal supremacy. As Luther told Melanchthon, "Agreement on doctrine is plainly impossible, unless the pope will abolish his popedom." By autumn, the situation seemed so hopeless that the Lutherans withdrew from the Diet, which then proceeded to confirm the Edict of Worms and demanded that all

Philip Melanchthon

Protestants should return to the Church. Nevertheless, the Diet of Augsburg marked an important milestone in the development of the Lutheran church; the Confession gave a broad statement of its beliefs. The failure of the attempts at religious pacification in Germany meant that the country was now divided between rival faiths, and the Lutheran church had gained a more secure position among the people.

It soon became clear that religious disunity was likely to produce dangerous political discord in Germany. In 1531, eight princes of the Empire and the representatives of eleven free cities formed the League of Schmalkalden (named after the town on the borders of Hesse and Saxony where they met) for the defense of Lutheranism. They agreed to assist one another if any one of them should be attacked, "on account of the Word of God and the doctrine of the Gospel." But there was no such immediate danger. Renewed war against France and a continuous threat to his lands from the Turks in the Balkans again prevented Charles from taking any action to enforce religious unity in Germany. The decisions of the Diet of Augsburg could have no effect. Differences of belief now had to be tolerated, and the League of Schmalkalden was accepted. Lutheranism was to continue to expand peacefully for the rest of Luther's life.

8

Catechism and Hymns

In his earnest desire that all Christians should be instructed in
the teaching of their faith, Luther not only emphasized the
importance of university education for the clergy and sermons
for the laity. He also wanted to make sure that children received a good foundation in religious knowledge. To this end,
he wrote in 1529 his Small Catechism, which was a manual of
Christian doctrine. The Small Catechism was arranged so that
the lessons could be taught by a simple method of question
and answer. When Luther first thought of writing a Catechism, he said, "What we need first of all is a good plain Catechism . . . for such instruction I know no better form than
those three parts which have been preserved in the Christian
church from the beginning—the Ten Commandments, the
Creed, and the Lord's Prayer—which contain in brief sum-
mary all that a Christian ought to know." These three parts he
made the basis of his Catechism, and his interpretation of them

was simple, straightforward, and full of the joyful sense of liberation and hopeful new life he himself had come to know through his own religious experience.

This, for instance, is his commentary on the second article of the Creed:

> I believe that Jesus Christ is not only truly God, born of the Father from all eternity, but also truly man, born of the Virgin Mary; that He is my Lord, and has delivered and redeemed me from all my sins, from death and slavery to the devil, after I had been lost and damned. He has truly bought me, not with silver and gold, but with His precious blood. His sufferings and His innocent death, that I may belong entirely to Him, and, living under His rule, I may serve Him in justice, innocence and eternal happiness; as He, risen from the dead, lives and reigns for ever and ever. This I firmly believe.

Luther trusted that the Catechism would educate children firmly in the knowledge of the essentials of the Christian religion. He hoped that, if all his other writings were to perish, this would remain. To those people who criticized it as being too slight and short, he replied:

> Do not think that Catechism is a little thing to be read hastily and cast aside. Although I am a doctor, I have to do just as a child and say word for word every morning and whenever I have the time the Lord's Prayer and the Ten Commandments, the Creed and the Psalms. I have to do it every day, and yet I cannot stand as I would. But these smart folk in one reading want to be doctors of doctors. Therefore I beg these wise saints to be persuaded that they are not such great doctors as they think. To be occupied with God's Word helps against the world, the flesh and the devil and all bad thoughts. This is the true holy water with which to exorcise the devil.

When it was printed, the Catechism was illustrated with quaint little woodcuts of Biblical and other scenes to help the

Luther preaching—from a manuscript of his prayers

children understand the points of the teaching. The first article of the Creed, "I believe in God the Father Almighty, Maker of Heaven and Earth," was accompanied by a picture of God creating the world and its animals. "Hallowed be thy name," from the Lord's Prayer, was illustrated by a preacher in a pulpit with a small congregation listening to his sermon. The illustration for the Fourth Commandment, "Remember the Sabbath," showed a service in a church, while outside, an irreligious man gathered firewood. The woodcut for the Tenth Commandment, "Thou shalt not covet thy neighbour's wife," depicted David, with his harp, coyly looking at Bathsheba, who was modestly having her feet washed.

Luther thought that the clergy might draw upon the Catechism as the basis for some of their sermons in church, but, more particularly, he intended it for use in the home. He wanted there to be a catechetical hour once a week in every home. Fathers should teach the Catechism to their children, and housewives to their servant girls, making them learn by heart the answers to the questions. Children who would not learn should have no food until they did; servants who refused it should be dismissed. At the end of the catechetical hour, Luther proposed that a psalm or hymn be sung.

Luther believed that hymns had an important part to play, together with Bible-reading, preaching, and catechizing, in sustaining and enriching the religious life of the people. He wrote:

I am strongly persuaded that, after theology, there is no art that can be placed on a level with music; for besides theology, music is the only art capable of affording peace and joy of the heart like that induced by the study of the science of divinity. A proof of this is that the devil, the originator of sorrowful anxieties and restless troubles, flees before the sound of music almost as much as before the Word of God.

Luther never lost the love of music he had shown in his student days, when he sang with his friends and learned to

A contemporary print showing an imaginary scene in which Luther (*left*) and Huss (*right*) administer communion to members of the House of Saxony

play the lute. He said, "My heart bubbles up and overflows in response to music, which has so often refreshed me and delivered me from dire plagues." He also remembered his earlier boyhood years when he had sung in the church choir. He always approved of the use of professional choirs in religious worship and was sorry when the new Elector, John Frederick, who had succeeded his father, the Elector John, in 1532, economized by discontinuing the choir. This choir had sung in the Parish Church and at the court in Wittenberg since the days of the generous Elector Frederick the Wise.

Luther also loved to hear the congregation sing in church. As the years went by, he became greatly interested in the national and traditional songs he heard German laborers and housewives sing at their work. Their simplicity and beauty charmed him. He wanted the new German hymns to be sung to tunes based on these songs as well as the old Latin chants. "It is my intention to make German psalms for the people," he wrote, "Spiritual songs, that is, whereby the Word of God may be kept alive in them by singing."

When these hymns had been written, the people soon learned to sing them. Children were taught to sing them in school, and there was regular hymn practice in the churches during the week for the congregation. An opponent of the Reformation said, "The German people sang themselves into heresy." Indeed, people were brought to Lutheranism as much through singing as through sermons.

This is what happened in Magdeburg during the early days of the Reformation; it was told by the chronicler of the city:

> On the day of St. John, between Easter and Pentecost, an old man, a weaver, came through the city gate to the monument of the Emperor Otto and there offered hymns for sale while he sang them to the people. The burgomaster, coming from early

mass and seeing the crowd, asked one of his servants what was going on. "There is an old rogue over there," he answered, "who is singing and selling the hymns of the heretic Luther." The burgomaster had the old man arrested and thrown into prison, but 200 citizens interceded, and he was released.

The first Lutheran hymnbook appeared in 1524. It was a small collection of eight German hymns of which four were by Luther himself. Soon afterward, he published twenty-four more of his own hymns, and later he wrote twelve more. Luther did not, therefore, write very many hymns. He wrote them only when he felt inspired to do so, and his hymns consequently express in sincere, simple terms his heartfelt religious experiences in words of praise. One of them, for instance, reflects the despair of his early life but then describes God's longing love for the world and the joyful acceptance by Christ of His mission. Christ, introduced as speaking to the hymn-writer, says:

> For I am with thee, thou art Mine,
> Henceforth My place is also thine,
> The foe shall never part us.

> I know that he will shed My blood,
> And take My life away;
> But I will bear it for thy good,
> Only believe alway.

> Death swallows up this life of Mine,
> My innocence all sins of thine,
> And so art thou delivered.

The same theme was also expressed in another of Luther's hymns, based on Psalm 130, *Aus tiefer Not*. This was among

the hymns which the old hymn-singer sang through the streets
of Magdeburg to the people as they came out of church from
mass on a saint's day, and it was to be sung at Luther's funeral:

> Out of the depths I cry to Thee
> Lord God, oh hear my prayer,
> Incline a gracious ear to me,
> And bid me not despair:
> If Thou rememberest each misdeed,
> If each should have its rightful meed,
> Lord, who shall stand before Thee?
>
> 'Tis through Thy love alone we gain
> The pardon of our sin;
> The strictest life is but in vain,
> Our words can nothing win,
> That none should boast himself of aught,
> But own in fear Thy grace hath wrought
> What in him seemeth righteous.
>
> Wherefore my hope is in the Lord,
> My works I count but dust,
> I build not there, but on His word,
> And in His goodness trust.
> Up to His care myself I yield,
> He is my tower, my rock, my shield,
> And for His help I tarry.

Very different from these two hymns is the little Christmas
carol *Vom Himmel hoch da komm ich her*, called by Luther
"a child's Christmas song concerning the child Jesus" and
written by him in 1540 for his little boy Hans:

> From heaven above to earth I come
> To bear good news to every home;

Glad tidings of great joy I bring,
Whereof I now will say and sing:

To you this night is born a child
Of Mary, chosen mother mild;
This little child of lowly birth
Shall be the joy of all your earth.

Give heed, my heart, lift up thine eyes!
Who is it in yon manger lies?
Who is this child so young and fair?
The blessed Christ-child lieth there.

Were earth a thousand times as fair,
Beset with gold and jewels rare,
She yet were far too poor to be
A narrow cradle, Lord, for Thee.

By far the most famous and best-known of Luther's hymns, however, is the great *Ein' feste Burg ist unser Gott*, which was translated into English by Thomas Carlyle and has been called the battle song of the Reformation. In it, Luther expressed his conviction of man's powerlessness, when left to himself, and his faith in the omnipotence of God, Who works through Christ. Sustained by this faith, he felt no superstitious terror but only confident, joyful defiance because he trusted in the triumphant Christ, the great conqueror. And so he ended the hymn with the assurance that the creative and saving Word that is Christ Himself would triumph over the accumulated might of sin and death:

A safe stronghold our God is still,
A trusty shield and weapon;
He'll help us clear from all the ill
That hath us now o'ertaken.

The hymn "A Safe Stronghold" in Luther's hand

The ancient prince of hell
Hath risen with purpose fell;
Strong mail of craft and power
He weareth in this hour;
On earth is not his fellow.

With force of arms we nothing can,
Full soon were we down-ridden;
But for us fights the proper Man,
Whom God himself hath bidden.
Ask ye, who is this same?

Christ Jesus is his name,
The Lord Sabaoth's Son;
He and no other one
Shall conquer in the battle.

And were this world all devils o'er,
And watching to devour us,
We lay it not to heart so sore;
Not they can overpower us.
And let the prince of ill
Look grim as e'er he will,
He harms us not a whit;
For why his doom is writ;
A word shall quickly slay him.

God's word, for all their craft and force,
One moment will not linger,
But, spite of hell, shall have its course;
'Tis written by his finger.
And though they take our life,
Goods, honor, children, wife,
Yet it is their profit small;
These things shall vanish all:
The City of God remaineth.

It is not certain when Luther wrote this hymn. It may have been in 1529 during the Diet of Speyer, when the famous Protestation was made, or it may have been a year or two earlier, when Lutherans were enduring persecution in southern Germany, and a Bavarian pastor, Leonard Kaiser, was burned alive. Carlyle said that the hymn was "like the sound of Alpine avalanches or the first murmur of earthquakes." With its rugged, majestic tune, which was also composed by Luther, it quickly spread throughout Germany.

Luther himself sang it daily while staying in the Castle of

Coburg during the anxious days of the Diet of Augsburg. In 1547, the year after Luther's death, when religious troubles brought Melanchthon temporary banishment from Wittenberg, he was cheered by hearing a little girl singing the hymn as he came into Weimar. And in the seventeenth century, when the terrible Thirty Years' War raged in Germany, Gustavus Adolphus of Sweden, the leader of the Protestant side, had it sung by his whole army as they were drawn up in array, prior to the Battle of Leipzig in 1631.

Nor was the influence of the hymn confined to Germany. During the first part of the eighteenth century, a group of Protestants, the Moravian Brethren, who traced their origins back to the teachings of Johannes Huss, were persecuted in Bohemia by the imperial authorities. A number of the Brethren assembled one day in 1723 to worship in a private house. An imperial officer was sent to seize their books and dismiss their assembly, but when he entered the house of the Brethren, all stood and sang *Ein' feste Burg*.

Many of the Brethren were arrested and imprisoned during the persecution, but some escaped and emigrated to the new English colony of Georgia in North America. The ship in which they crossed the Atlantic encountered such a fearful storm that all on board were terrified except the Brethren themselves, who calmly spent the time in prayer and worship. Also in the ship was young John Wesley, who was to make an unsuccessful attempt to work as a missionary among the Indians in the colony. Wesley was so impressed by the confident, courageous, hymn-singing of the Brethren that he could not believe himself a Christian in comparison with them and longed to know the secret of their faith.

9

Marriage and Later Years

For a long time it had been a common practice among the nobility for parents to send their daughters into a convent if they did not wish to find husbands for them and provide them with a dowry, or did not have the means to do so. At the Cistercian convent of Nimptschen, near Grimma in Saxony, there were a number of girls of good birth who had been placed there for this reason. One of them was Catherine von Bora, who belonged to an ancient and noble family. When she was a young girl, her father had married for the second time and sent her to Nimptschen, where one of her aunts was the abbess, and another a nun. Though her aunt was a strict abbess and punished troublesome novices with the rod and several days on a diet of bread and water, she could not make Catherine into a good nun. Catherine found life in the convent increasingly irksome and longed for freedom.

After reading several of Luther's books, which had been

A portrait by Cranach of Luther's wife

smuggled into the convent, Catherine became convinced that
it would not be sinful for her to relinquish the veil. She discussed the matter with eleven other young ladies who also
wanted to leave the convent, and they decided to plan their
escape. They probably managed to get in touch with Luther;
a follower of his, the sixty-year-old merchant Leonard Koppe
of Torgau, who supplied the convent with herrings, agreed to
take them away secretly in one of his covered wagons. On the
night of Good Friday, 1523, he brought the twelve nuns, who

lay on the floor of the wagon, hidden between herring barrels, through the hostile territory of Duke George of Saxony to Torgau. Three of the girls were taken back by their parents, but the remaining nine (including Catherine) either were not wanted or could not go home because their families lived in Duke George's part of Saxony. They were taken on to Wittenberg. "A wagonload of vestal virgins has just come to town, all more eager for marriage than for life," a student told a friend. "God grant them husbands lest a worst befall."

Luther felt responsible for them and placed them in service with friendly people in Wittenberg. Within two years, all were married except Catherine. She was still working as a domestic servant in the house of the burgomaster whose wife was strict; and in those days, maidservants also might expect to be whipped with the birch rod if their work did not satisfy their mistress. Catherine received excellent training in her position, but she liked it no more than she had the convent. She longed for a household of her own to manage and would gladly have taken a husband, particularly as she was well past the age at which most girls married. Though Luther was now distracted by the events of the Peasants' Revolt, he readily did what he could to help her, but without success. A well-to-do student courted her, but when his family pointed out that it would hardly be to his advantage to marry a penniless, runaway nun, he withdrew. Others, whom Luther suggested, were not acceptable to her. At last, she frankly told a professor of the university that she would like to marry him or even Luther himself.

Luther had the year before laid aside his friar's habit and wore now a plain grey coat made from a length of broadcloth given to him by Archduke John. He now considered himself free to marry and believed he would get married some day.

When Catherine's remark was reported to him, he at first treated it as a joke; but he knew that his father had long wanted him to get married so that he could have grandchildren. Luther, therefore, took Catherine's suggestion as a sign that she was intended to be his wife, though he could not pretend that he was in love with her. Catherine, in her turn, at first thought his proposal a jest, but she soon saw that he was in earnest and readily accepted him. They were married in June, 1525, and Luther took his bride back to the old priory. He was forty-two years old, and Catherine twenty-six.

Luther's opponents scoffed at the marriage. Erasmus said that Luther's career had begun as a tragedy and now ended as a comedy; but Luther had come to believe that marriage and a home were the life intended by God for most people, and he wanted to try to set an example of good Christian family life. Luther's new circumstances brought changes in his habits. "Before I was married," he said, "the bed was not made for a whole year and became foul with sweat; but I worked so hard and was so weary that I tumbled in without noticing it." The neat, well-trained Catherine put an end to that and kept the priory cleaner than it had been for a long time. He himself reflected, "There is a lot to get used to in the first year of marriage. One wakes up in the morning and finds a pair of pigtails on the pillow which were not there before." During these months, Catherine did her best to make him acquire more regular habits and to abandon his way of mending his own clothes by cutting out a good patch of cloth from another garment.

For Catherine, indeed, the marriage brought even greater changes. Instead of being a servant girl, she now had her own servants and household to manage, and this was not an easy task. The unfinished building of the Augustinian priory did not exactly make an ideal home. It had many small cells, but few large rooms. Even though the Elector John had doubled Luther's salary as a professor after the marriage, it was still small, and Luther's only possessions were his books and his clothes. He refused to accept any money for the widely selling books he was writing, though they probably would have made him a wealthy man. "What I have got for nothing," he said, "I will give for nothing." His publishers made their fortunes, while he and his wife (and later their family) never found it easy to make ends meet.

Yet, whatever their problems, neither Luther nor his wife were ever daunted by them and did not claim sympathy; they were supremely happy in their marriage. If he was not in love when he proposed to her, he soon was very much so. To him she was "Katie," and he sometimes even made a pun upon it and called her his "*Kette*" (which in German means "chain").

The courtyard of the Augustinian priory at Wittenberg, where Luther at one time lived

Her portrait shows that she was not exactly handsome, but it does suggest that she was cheerful, prepossessing, and good-humored. After a year of married life, Luther told a friend, "My Katie is in all things so obliging and pleasing to me that I would not exchange my poverty for the riches of Croesus."

Catherine did not resent the fact that she was entirely over-shadowed by her famous husband, and that people came to talk with him and not with her. She always called him "Doctor" and curtsied to him in public. Today, their home is a museum and still has the fine doorway of sandstone which was a present to Luther from Catherine. It bears his coat of arms and portrait with the words "He [Christ] lives," and "In quietness and confidence shall be your strength."

Both husband and wife took their part in the affairs of the household. Luther worked in the priory garden, growing lettuces and cabbages, peas and beans, cucumbers and melons. Catherine was responsible for a small farm outside the town, which included an orchard and a fish-pond; the farm provided apples and pears, grapes and peaches, trout and pike, hens and ducks, pigs and cows. Catherine caught the fish and even slaughtered the cattle herself, besides making butter, drying herbs, and brewing beer. In a letter, which he wrote in 1535, Luther said, "My lord Katie greets you. She plants our fields and pastures, sells cows, *et cetera*."

Among the other things Catherine did was to redecorate a few of the rooms that had formerly been cells and take in students as boarders to make a little more money, but Luther could never refuse hospitality or accommodation to anyone whether they could pay or not. Even on their wedding night, when Luther and his wife had parted from the guests at the banquet at eleven o'clock, Karlstadt had come knocking at their door; he had been driven from his parish by the Peasants'

Revolt, and Luther, who had previously done his best to make him leave Wittenberg, gave him shelter for a time.

Throughout their married life, there were always other people to care for. Among their numerous temporary guests were monks and nuns who had fled from the cloister and Protestant ministers driven from their churches. And during a time of plague in Wittenberg, Luther took in several children who had lost their parents. He also kept a free table for poor students. The priory was suitable for use as a hospital or almshouse, and he took in the sick and needy and supported them at his own expense. When Catherine protested once, as she saw him again giving money to a beggar, he replied, "Dear Kate, God is rich. He will give us some more." And to a friend he said, "We ought to give freely, simply, of pure love, willingly." Later, their own children came to add to the numbers of the household, which on occasions included as many as twenty-five people.

A picture of Luther's home is drawn in a letter to Prince George of Anhalt, written by someone who was advising him not to spend a night there:

> The home of Luther is occupied by a motley crowd of boys, students, girls, widows, old women, and youngsters. For this reason there is much disturbance in the place, and many regret it for the sake of the good man, the honorable father. If only the spirit of Doctor Luther lived in all of these, his house would offer you an agreeable, friendly quarter for a few days so that your Grace would be able to enjoy the hospitality of that man. But as the situation now stands and as circumstances exist in the household of Luther, I would not advise your Grace to stay there.

All sorts of games were played in the priory. Luther set up a bowling alley in the garden. He himself liked an occasional game of chess, but his favorite diversion was still music and singing. He sang and played the lute as he had done in his student days, and students who had training in music were especially welcome in his house.

Luther and his wife had six children, three boys and three girls; they also brought up four young orphaned relatives. The arrival of children added to their problems, but Luther said, "These are the joys of marriage of which the pope is not worthy." When their first child was born in July, 1526, Luther told his friends, "A Lutheran has come!" When, in accordance with the custom of the time, the baby was wrapped up tightly in swaddling clothes and cried loudly, Luther, who was standing by, said, "Cry away! Kick away! The pope wrapped me up too, but I kicked his bindings off." Although he insisted on obedience from his children and punished them when they misbehaved, he purposely did not treat them as harshly as his parents had treated him. There were rewards as well as punishments. "If you give lickings," he said, "keep an apple in sight as well as the rod." He reveled in the children's company, sometimes joining in their games, and was proud of their achievements.

Indeed, Luther thoroughly enjoyed family life. As the years went by, he became more relaxed and cheerful. The formerly lean, ascetic, troubled friar grew fat and contented and looked more like one of his German peasant-farmer ancestors than a university professor. Though he refused to recognize fasting as a "good work," he sometimes lived day after day on nothing except bread and water, and his wife had difficulty in persuading him to eat more. But usually, he was a great eater as well as a great drinker and boasted of it. He said, "If our Lord found it right to create great pike and Rhenish wine, then we may take and use them." He also drank beer in the evening, as was customary at that time. He had a large beer mug around which were engraved three rings. The first he described as representing the Ten Commandments; the second, the Apostles' Creed; and the third, the Lord's Prayer. He could always drink down to the Lord's Prayer and was amused if a guest tried to emulate him and could only get as far as the Ten Commandments. Yet even his enemies could never claim that he drank too much.

Luther enjoyed the company that continually came to his house. He was now the most famous man in Germany. All sorts of people from different parts of the country as well as from abroad wanted to meet him. Since he kept such an open house, they were welcomed and often joined with the students in taking meals with him. On these occasions, Luther readily talked and answered questions on a hundred and one different topics. Some people sat at the table with notebooks and copied down his every word, which they later published as a huge volume called *Luther's Table Talk*. Here are a few of his sayings from it:

> Printing is God's latest and best work to spread the true religion throughout the world.—A dog is a most faithful animal and would be more highly prized if less common.—They are trying to make me into a fixed star, but I am an irregular planet.—Germany is the pope's pig. That is why we have to give him so much bacon and sausages.

Not that Luther was at all idle during these years. He was still a professor at the university and gave his lectures regularly. He was in constant demand as a preacher at neighboring churches and also as a counselor, when problems arose in the parishes. He engaged in disputes with opponents as energetically as ever, and his language became even less restrained than before. His correspondence was voluminous and continual, because people wrote to him on innumerable questions and had to be answered. In addition, he composed his hymns and prayers for the people. All this did not distract him from caring for the religious education of his own family. Every Sunday evening, he preached in the former priory chapel to all who were in his house, and one New Year's Day he offered Catherine a sum of money if she would read through the Bible by Easter.

Year after year, Luther went on preaching and lecturing, writing and advising. His home was still full of all sorts of people, and Catherine continued to complain that she could not find her way about because of the papers and books that were everywhere. His energy and enthusiasm endured until the last years of his life, when he was overtaken by ill-health and weariness. His nerves became frayed and his spirits low. "I am," he said, "exhausted with age and work—old, cold, and out of shape—and yet I am not allowed to rest, but daily tormented with all manner of business and the toil of scribbling."

Moreover, Luther now seemed unable to deal with some of the problems which faced him. The most notorious of these was the case of Philip of Hesse. As a young man, Philip had been married, for political reasons, to Duke George's daughter. The marriage soon proved unhappy, and, until his conversion to Lutheranism, Philip lived in immorality. In 1540, he wished to divorce his wife and marry again. Although Luther firmly upheld the permanence of marriage, in the end he had to agree to allow Philip to take a second wife. He unrealistically hoped that his marriage would remain secret and even told Philip to "tell a good strong lie for the sake and good of the Christian Church." But inevitably, the bigamy could not be concealed, and it became a reproach to the Protestant movement.

As early as 1531, Luther said, "I have lived long enough.

Not until I am gone will they feel Luther's full weight." It was depressing and exasperating for him to feel more and more that his work was really over. A new generation of younger men was taking control of Lutheranism in Germany. They held Luther in the highest esteem, but no longer was his advice sought far and wide. Even in Wittenberg, his practical influence faded. He did not like it and came to believe that the course of events was taking a steady turn for the worse. When the Princess Elizabeth of Brandenburg, whom he visited at Lichtenburg in June, 1539, wished him forty more years of life, he replied that the world was so wicked, he could wish "for nothing better than one blessed hour and then departure to the next."

These times when he despaired of the world cast him into deep gloom. In April, 1543, he said, "Everywhere the license and impudence of the people increase. The magistrates are to blame, for they do nothing except exact taxes. The governments have become institutions for the ingathering of treasures and taxes. Therefore the Lord will destroy us in His anger. Would that the day of our redemption would quickly come!" Yet, whenever he was in such a mood, if a call came to him from someone in need, he would at once forget his worries and do what he could to help.

This is what happened at the end of his life. In the autumn of 1545, he saw some young women in Wittenberg wearing such low-cut dresses that he was filled with disgust and left home, avowing that he would not return. His physician brought him back. That winter, a plea arrived from the counts of Mansfeld for a mediator to come and settle a family quarrel. Melanchthon was too ill to go, so Luther undertook the long and tiring winter journey. By the middle of February he had reconciled the counts. On the way back, he preached at Eisleben, where he had been born. He ended his sermon much sooner than usual, saying to the congregation, "Much more needs to be said about this passage in the gospel, but I do not feel strong enough just now, and so the matter must rest there."

He died of a heart attack four days later, on February 18, 1546, in Eisleben. The next day, the funeral service was held in St. Andrew's Church, where he had been baptized over sixty-two years before. Archduke John Frederick wanted him to be buried in Wittenberg. His body was taken there, a journey of eighty miles, over the wintry roads of the Thuringian Forest. In all the towns and villages through which his coffin passed, the church bells tolled, and large crowds paid him their last respects. In the city of Halle, the coffin was carried into the parish church. The congregation wept during the singing of Psalm 130, "Out of the depths I have cried to Thee," which Luther himself had translated and put into German verse. Then the leading citizens kept watch by the coffin throughout the night.

When the hearse arrived in Wittenberg, students carried the coffin through the door of the Castle Church on which the Ninety-five Theses had been nailed. Martin Luther was buried in a grave near the pulpit from which he had so often preached.

Two days before he died, Luther had inscribed a friend's book with a text from St. John's Gospel: "If anyone obeys my teaching, he shall never know what it is to die." And he added, "How incredible is such a text, and yet it is the truth. If a man takes God's word in full earnest and believes in it and then falls asleep, he slips away without noticing death and is safe on the other side."

IO

Epilogue

Between 1520 and 1560, some 16,000 students came to the University of Wittenberg to study the teachings of Luther, Melanchthon, and their successors in the theological faculty. About a third of these students came from northern Germany; a third, from southern Germany; and a third, from foreign countries. After completing their studies, they left again to become active missionaries for the beliefs of Lutheranism in their homelands all over Europe. Assisting them in their efforts to spread the ideas of Lutheranism was the printing press. Lutheranism was the first great movement to reach the minds of men through the printed word, and Luther understood and appreciated its power. When one of his followers zealously urged the Wittenberg theologians to go out into the world to preach their message to the people, Luther replied, "We do that with our books."

Carried by men and by books, the ideas first proclaimed by Luther rapidly spread not only in Germany and other European countries but throughout the world. The new ideas of the Reformation traveled across the frontiers into Switzerland and France, the Netherlands and the Hapsburg lands, and over the waters to Scandinavia and to England and Scotland. Later, they went with men and women who were seeking new homes in the lands across the Atlantic. These ideas were molded and developed by other thinkers and reformers, who made changes and developed forms of organization very different from those proposed by Luther. Zwingli and Calvin in Switzerland, Cranmer in England, and Knox in Scotland— these were some of the men who first took the lead in shaping Protestantism in these countries.

Many of these religious leaders in other lands came to hold beliefs different from Luther's. But, to all of them, his example and teaching had provided the first inspiration. Nowhere was this more evident than in England. Luther's books were eagerly welcomed and discussed by a small group of scholars at Cambridge University.* One of them was William Tyndale, who was determined to translate the Bible into English and to make known the teachings of Luther in England. Luther had written prefaces for his German Bible to explain the meaning of its books, and Tyndale put into English Luther's Preface to the Epistle to the Romans and included it in his New Testament. He also translated and incorporated much of the other prefaces from Luther's Bible.

Tyndale disguised Luther's works so well that no one in England traced them to their heretical source. In 1538, Henry VIII, who by this time had quarreled with the papacy, author-

* See p. 3.

ized that an English translation of the Bible be read in England's churches. It would indeed have shocked King Henry had he known that Luther's prefaces were included in that Bible, for he never overcame his dislike of Luther's views. But, through Luther's prefaces, the English people were given the opportunity of reading the ideas of the Protestant Reformation as well as the Scriptures.

In England, as in many other countries, there was at this time much dissatisfaction with the services of the Church. The people did not participate actively in the services. The worship in the parish churches followed the Latin breviary, the book containing the daily services for the monks which Luther found so unsatisfactory.* Even conservative people in England thought that these services should be shortened and simplified. But one of England's parties wanted to follow the Lutheran example and replace these Latin services with English ones in which the people could take part. Henry VIII, however, sided with the conservatives. There is in the British Museum a manuscript, in the handwriting of Archbishop Cranmer, containing two schemes for amending the Latin services of the breviary.

King Henry's death in 1547 freed the Archbishop from all restriction. He now associated himself with the party that favored the Lutheran reforms, and two years later he produced a new book of services in the English language—the Book of Common Prayer, which is still used today by the Church of England and the Protestant Episcopal church of the United States.

Moreover, long after Luther's death, his influence was ex-

* See p. 27.

erted in a remarkable way in eighteenth-century England. When John Wesley returned from Georgia, he had not forgotten the profound impression made upon him by the Moravian Brethren.* In London, one May evening in 1738, he went to a meeting in a house in Aldersgate Street held by Moravian exiles in England. There, a member of the Brethren was reading aloud Luther's Preface to the Epistle to the Romans. Wesley afterward wrote in his *Journal,* "while he was describing the change which God works in the heart through faith in Christ, I felt my heart strangely warmed. I felt I did trust in Christ, Christ alone, for salvation." It was the same assurance of personal salvation through Christ that Luther himself had experienced over two centuries earlier, and this experience had the same effect upon Wesley's life.

John Wesley devoted the rest of his life "to promote as far as I am able vital practical religion and by the grace of God to beget, preserve and increase the life of God in the souls of men." The result of his labors was the establishment of Methodism, the largest of all the Protestant sects.

Luther himself, when he first came to trust in his own salvation and then went on to attack the abuses of the papacy, could not, of course, have foreseen these consequences of his words and deeds. His hope had been to lead all men to Christ and purge the Church of corruption. He had no wish to split the Church, but the division he had initiated was perpetuated in the year before his death, at the meetings of the Council of Trent. Luther and other reformers had hoped that a council of the Church might bring about the changes they desired, but this council, when at last summoned by the papacy to the city of Trent, displayed no spirit of compromise and set out to

* See p. 100.

define, beyond a doubt, the ways in which Roman Catholicism differed from Protestantism. And so in Germany and beyond, Christians were divided between those who continued to accept papal authority and those who rejected it.

This was the price of Luther's protest. But it had also brought about great gains. Before he had made his stand, the human spirit and conscience seemed to be in great danger of becoming estranged from God because of the materialism and worldliness that had characterized the medieval Church.

Luther brought men a fresh conception of God's grace and sovereignty. He swept away the irrelevant and harmful accumulations of centuries and compelled people to concentrate on what really mattered. For none, whether Protestant or Roman Catholic, could religion ever be the same again in the years to come. He had provided to all Christians a fresh vision, which was to lead them forward to more new ideas and ventures in the future.

The Main Events in Luther's Life

1483. Born at Eisleben.
1484. The family moved to Mansfeld.
1497. Went to school at Magdeburg.
1498. Changed to St. George's School in Eisenach.
1501–5. Became a student at the University of Erfurt.
1502. The University of Wittenberg founded.
1505. Became an Augustinian friar.
1507. Ordained to the priesthood.
1508. Lectured at Wittenberg.
1510. Visited Rome.
1512. Became a professor at Wittenberg.
1513–15. Lectured on the Psalms.
1515–16. Lectured on the Epistle to the Romans.
1516–17. Lectured on the Epistle to the Galatians.
1517. Published his "Ninety-five Theses" against indulgences.
1517–18. Lectured on the Epistle to the Hebrews.

1518. Interviewed by Cardinal Cajetan at Augsburg.
Melanchthon become a professor at Wittenberg.
1519. Disputation with Eck at Leipzig.
Charles V elected Holy Roman Emperor.
1520. Published: *To the Christian Nobility of the German Nation, On the Babylonian Captivity of the Church, Of the Liberty of a Christian Man.* Papal bull *Exsurge Domine* condemned Luther's heresies.
Burning of the papal bull at Wittenberg.
1521. Excommunicated by the papal bull *Dicet Romanum Pontificem.*
Diet and Edict of Worms.
Death of Pope Leo X.
1521–22. Concealment at Wartburg Castle.
1522. Completed translation of New Testament into German and returned to Wittenberg.
1524. Abandoned the habit of the Augustinian friars.
1524–25. The Peasants' Revolt.
1525. Married Catherine von Bora.
Dispute with Erasmus.
Frederick the Wise succeeded by his brother, John.
1526. Publication of Luther's German mass.
1529. Diet and Protestation of Speyer.
Colloquy of Marburg.
Publication of Luther's Catechism.
1530. Diet and Confession of Augsburg.
1531. Formation of the League of Schmalkalden.
1532. Elector John of Saxony succeeded by John Frederick.
1534. Completed translation of Old Testament into German.
1545. Opening of the Council of Trent.
1546. Luther's death.

Suggestions for Further Reading

The following books contain a great deal of information about Luther's European and German background and about his career:

G. R. ELTON, *Reformation Europe 1517–1550* (New York: Torchbooks, Harper & Row, 1966; paperback).

PRESERVED SMITH, *The Age of the Reformation* (New York: Collier Books, 1962; 2 vols., paperback).

The books listed below describe the course of the Reformation as a whole.

OWEN CHADWICK, *The Reformation* (Baltimore, Md.: Penguin Books, 1964; paperback).

L. W. COWIE, *The Reformation* (London: Young Historian Books, Weidenfeld & Nicolson, 1967).

A. G. DICKENS, *Reformation and Society in Sixteenth-Century Europe* (New York: Harcourt, Brace & World, 1966; paperback).

NORMAN SYKES, *The Crisis of the Reformation* (Naperville, Ill.: Alec R. Allenson, 1951. New York: W. W. Norton, 1966; paperback).

Here is an excellent book on Luther's life:

R. H. BAINTON, *Here I Stand* (New York: Mentor Books, New American Library, 1955; paperback).

Index

Against the Murdering, Thieving Hordes of the Peasants, 73
Albert, Archbishop of Mainz, 40, 44–45, 60
Albrecht of Hohenzollern, 78
Aleandro, Cardinal, 57–58, 60
Anabaptists, 74
Anne, St., 25
Antwerp, 64
Augsburg, 4, 6, 45, 78; Confession of, 86–87; Diet of, 85, 87–88, 100
Augustine, St., 38, 48
Augustinian Order, 25, 26–36, 45, 64, 67, 69, 71

Bible, 63, 69, 114
Bohemia, 6, 100
Boniface VIII, Pope, 40
Book of Common Prayer, 115
Bora, Catherine von; *see* Luther, Catherine
Brandenburg-Ansbach, Margrave of, 78, 85
Bremen, 78
Brothers of the Common Life, 19–20
Brunswick, Duke of, 74, 78

Cajetan, Cardinal, 45–46
Calvin, John, 114
Cambridge University, 114
Campeggio, Cardinal, 86
Carlyle, Thomas, 97, 99
Catholic Church, 8–14, 32–35, 37–51, 54, 59–60, 84, 116
Charlemagne, Emperor of the West, 6–7
Charles V, Holy Roman Emperor, 8, 50, 53–54, 57–60, 64, 77, 84–86, 88
Cistercian convent of Nimptschen, 101
Coburg, Castle of, 85, 99–100
Cologne, 10, 50
Communion, 49, 65, 66, 69, 81–84
Confession of Augsburg, 86–87
Constance, Council of, 56
Cranach, Lucas, 5
Cranmer, Thomas, 4, 114–15

Decet Pontificem Romanum, 53
Dürer, Albrecht, 5

Eck, Johann von, 46–48, 50–51
Eckhart, Meister, 12, 35
Edict of Worms, 59, 64, 84, 86–87
Eisenach, 21, 60–62, 64, 67, 85
Eisleben, 15, 21, 112
Elizabeth, Princess of Brandenburg, 111
England, 114–16
Erasmus, Desiderius, 14, 20, 30, 63, 74–75, 104
Erfurt, 22, 51, 56; University of, 22–25
Exsurge Domine, 50–52

Francis I, King of France, 53–54
Franciscan friars, 21, 62
Frankenhausen, 74
Frederick of Saxony, 10, 29, 42, 44, 53, 56, 60, 66, 77
Frederick the Wise, 94

George, Duke of Saxony, 28, 46, 103
George, Prince of Anhalt, 107
Gustavus Adolphus, King of Sweden, 100

Hamburg, 78
Hanseatic League, 4, 20
Hapsburg family, 53, 114
Heidelberg, 45
Helfenstein, Count of, 73
Henry VIII, King of England, 3–4, 49, 114–15
Hesse, 74, 80; Landgrave of, 78
Holy Roman Empire, 6–8, 50, 53
Huss, Johannes, 12, 48, 53, 56, 100

Ingolstadt, 46
Innocent VIII, Pope, 39

John, Archduke of Saxony, 77, 94, 105
John Frederick, Archduke of Saxony, 94, 105, 112

121

John the Baptist, 9
Julius II, Pope, 40

Kaiser, Leonard, 99
Karlstadt, Andreas, 65–69, 81, 106
Knox, John, 114
Koppe, Leonard, 102

Latin language, 11, 18, 22, 52
League of Schmalkalden, 88
Leipzig, 29, 46, 51
Leo X, Pope, 40, 43–46, 50–51, 53
Liège, Luther's books burnt in, 50
Louvain, 50
Lupfen, Countess of, 71–72
Luther, Catherine, 101–10
Luther, Hans, 4, 15–18, 22, 24–25
Luther, Margaret, 15–18
Lutheranism, 63, 65–67, 69, 77–88, 89, 113
Luther's Table Talk, 109

Magdeburg, 19–21, 78, 94–96
Mansfeld, 15–19, 23, 24; counts of, 22, 78, 111–12
Marburg, 80, 82, 84; University of, 80
Martin of Tours, St., 15, 46
Mary; *see* Virgin Mary
Maximilian I, Holy Roman Emperor, 53
Melanchthon, Philip, 38, 48, 65–66, 68, 86–87, 100, 112, 113
Methodism, 116
Miltitz, Carl von, 45–46
Mohrs, 60
Moravian Brethren, 100, 116

Ninety-five Theses, 43–51, 112
Nuremberg, 6, 78

Oemler, Nicolas, 19
Of the Liberty of a Christian Man, 49
On Religious Vows, 67
On the Babylonian Captivity of the Church, 49

Papal bulls, 50–51, 53
Parker, Matthew, 4
Paul, St., 25, 58, 59; Epistles of, 30, 35–36, 37–38, 49–50, 114, 116
Peasants' Revolt, 71–74, 103, 107
Philip of Hesse, 82–84, 110
Protestantism, 84–86, 113–17
"Protestation" document, 84, 99

Prussia, 6, 78
Psalms, Luther lectures on, 30, 31

Reformation, 13–14, 37, 48, 78, 79, 80–83, 113–17
Renaissance, 13
Rome, Luther's visit to, 34

St. George's Church, Mansfeld, 19
St. George's School, Eisenach, 21
Saxony, 29, 74
Schleswig, Duke of, 78
Sixtus IV, Pope, 40
Small Catechism, 89–92
Speyer, Diet of, 84, 99
Staupitz, Johann von, 26–27, 29–30, 35, 74
Stotternheim, 24
Strasburg, 78
Stühlingen, 71–72

Tauler, Johannes, 35
Tetzel, Johann, 41–44
Thirty Years' War, 100
Three Treatises, 48
Thuringian Forest, 15, 21, 60, 62, 112
To the Christian Nobility of the German Nation, 48
Trebonius, Johann, 21
Trent, Council of, 116
Tyndale, William, 4, 114

University of Marburg, 80
University of Erfurt, 22–25
University of Wittenberg, 5, 29–35, 38, 48, 65, 80, 113

Virgin Mary, 9, 69

Wartburg Castle, Eisenach, 21, 60–63, 64, 67, 85
Weinsberg, massacre at, 73
Wesley, John, 100, 116
William, Prince of Anhalt, 20–21
Wittenberg, 10, 29, 43–44, 51, 52, 60, 64–71, 80, 94, 107, 112; *see also* University of Wittenberg
Worms, 54, 55–57; Diet of, 52–63, 85; Edict of, 59, 64, 84, 86–87
Wycliffe, John, 12

Zurich, 82
Zwickau, 68
Zwilling, Gabriel, 65, 66, 69
Zwingli, Ulrich, 82, 84, 114